Reviving the Classics Series

THE ROOT IS BITTER, THE ROOT IS SWEET

In the Shadow of Madness: a memoir

by Dolores Brandon

ORI Academic Press

Second Edition: Published in 2016 by
ORI Academic Press, New York, NY

First published in 2000 by Sky Blue Press, under the title:
IN THE SHADOW OF MADNESS: A Memoir

Printed in the United States of America on acid free paper.

Library of Congress Control Number: 2015961023

Cataloging Data:

Brandon, Dolores. The Root Is Bitter, the Root Is Sweet: In the Shadow
of Madness, a Memoir. (2nd edition)/ Dolores Brandon. [Reviving the
Classics Series]

1. Mental health, Family – Psychological aspects. 2. Psychobiography.
3. Intergenerational conflict –Unconscious communications.
4. Creativity (literary, artistic, etc.) – Psychological concepts.
5. Interracial marriage – Psychological concepts.

ISBN 978-1-942431-03-9 (soft cover)

Book cover art © 2015 by Marilyn Brandon

mindmendmedia
piecing it together

Book design & editing, - by MindMendMedia, Inc. @
MindMendMedia.com

In memory of my father and mother:

Alvin John Brandon   1913 –1973
Jeanne Julienne Brandon   1920 - 2013

Your courage, grace and bravery continue to inspire.

Connecting

Seeking answers in the dark pool of her heart
a sunflower blooms.

Yes,
she says,
the dark is filled with seeds
to be
scattered over the Earth.

Dolores Brandon
12.10.14

Publisher's Preface

I would like it to be thought that I had listened carefully to what patients and others have told me, that I've tried to imagine what it was like for them, and that I tried to convey this. And to use a biblical term, the feeling, 'he bore witness.'
— Oliver Sacks

Most of us, one way or another, are touched by mental or psycho-neurological illness - be it our school friend's petit-epileptic absent mindedness; or culturally unacceptable (although very soothing or coping) behaviors of our "on the spectrum" relatives, or the rollercoaster-felt daily experience of living with a bipolar-disordered parent, sibling, or child. And, although we became fairly good (and even good enough) in exercising empathic imagination and feeling the pain of an-Other, it is still not an easy task. It is not easy, not only because it takes an enormous effort, draining at times, – to FEEL like the Other – but because we also have our biases (mostly based on our upbringing, education, and acculturation), so our minds take a known path, and engage in a learned behavior of taking sides, and looking at everything from one specific position: this one is a victim, and this one - a perpetrator...

In her poignant and poetic account of living "in the shadow of madness" (her father's bipolar disorder), Dolores Brandon does the opposite. She does not take sides, and she does not ask us to take sides. She opens to us the world of love and horror, laughs and screams, joys and sorrows – happening all at the same time. So, we can truly say, "she bore witness." Dolores tells her story, not only masterfully, but with enormous kindness, sensitivity, and grace. She employs "simple" storytelling (what she calls *oral history*), and not so very simple poetry, inviting us all to experience her story ourselves.

By telling her story, Dolores also teaches us about the value of listening, without any judgment, preaching, and desire to "solve the problem" (which we are so much primed to do!). Her story also teaches us to be patient, and not afraid of being vulnerable, and even to wholeheartedly embrace vulnerability - as a symbol of hope and healing.

So, why this book, and why the 2nd edition? It is simply because this book is unique, in many ways. Like in the Wizard of Oz, everyone gets what's missing in their lives. For many families of "neuro-atypicals," it offers an alternative for suffering, despite all the pain and grief that are interwoven in this story's tapestry. For those who live with mental illness – it offers a hope to be understood and loved, no matter what. And for those in mental health field, it offers some insights and some alternatives to medicalization and pathologizing. As late Dr. Oliver Sacks, a great neuro-storyteller of all times, said once, *"A condition is sometimes a collusion, and sometimes a compromise,"* and that by getting into people's stories, we are getting into the *"interface of biography and biology, person and person-hood."*

The Root Is Bitter, The Root Is Sweet does just that! There is no other book that offers this kind of interface for ALL – patients and their families, educators, general medical practitioners, and mental health professionals. Besides all, Dolores Brandon achieves this by touching our souls, not just our minds. To re-phrase some of Oliver Sacks' last words of wisdom, Dolores Brandon was able to have *"an intercourse with the world, the special intercourse of writers and readers."*

— Inna Rozentsvit, M.D., PhD,
on behalf of ORI Academic Press
New York 2016

Author's Note to the 2nd Edition

When a book goes out of print, for the author it is as if a light is turned off in the chamber of the heart that gave it life. Yes, a vibrant used book market today keeps the distribution circuitry going, but it's not quite the same wattage. Opportunities to reach and grow one's audience are more random, often obscure and less supported. So, fifteen years after *IN THE SHADOW OF MADNESS* debuted under the imprimatur of *Sky Blue Press*, I welcomed the invitation *ORI Academic Press* extended to give this memoir a second edition. And, after some discussion, I agreed to have it republished with my original working title - *THE ROOT IS BITTER, THE ROOT IS SWEET* while retaining the title given the First Edition as subtitle. Although I grew to accept it, I was never entirely comfortable with *In the Shadow of Madness* as title: I felt it cast a pejorative pall on mental illness that was not part of my intention. My impulse for writing the book was born out of a need to unravel a legacy, to penetrate a personal genetic inheritance. Like Oliver Sachs, one of our truly great neurologist story tellers, I believe *"To be ourselves we must have ourselves – possess, if need be re-possess, our life-stories. We must "recollect" ourselves, recollect the inner drama, the narrative, of ourselves."*

Being published is typically a circuitous affair. I have been fortunate. Thanks to a brief, but nourishing personal association with diarist, Anais Nin, I met publisher, Paul Herron, just as he was laying in the foundation for *Sky Blue Press*. With his dedication to keeping the flame of Nin alive, Herron was open to considering the writings of Nin "offspring" for publication; in that context, my memoir caught his attention. I will be forever grateful to *Sky Blue Press* for the first edition and Herron's good wishes for this second one.

With its network of professionals and authors working to effect deeper, more compassionate avenues of public understanding for mental illness and the families who struggle to transcend its damages, *ORI Academic Press* feels like a good and right second home. I am profoundly grateful to Dr. Susan Kavaler-Adler and Dr. Inna Rozentsvit for their faith in the book and their choosing to republish it. And, I am once again thrilled to have my artist sister, Marilyn Brandon, create a new image for the cover of the new edition. We lived this experience together. She understands the book at its most personal level. The collage image she created is her visual *response* to the book's *call*.

Although it is ever more clear (to me, at least) that mental illness is at the very core of many of our contemporary world's most serious social problems, the plight of families as they struggle to cope with parents, siblings, wives and husbands so afflicted remains largely unvoiced. Every time I see a headline sensationalizing the tragic outcome of some disturbed person's anti-social behavior, I hear the muffled screams of a family standing in the shadows - the screams crying out for help, comfort and understanding; the screams that, if they were truly heard, could bring healing, safety and a sense of value to the lives of all so impacted.

The quality of response I received from readers to the first edition of this memoir tells me families want to be heard, that there's an audience deeply interested and ready to listen particularly when the stories are *unsugared* narratives of courage and compassion; stories frankly told by and about people who do not cave but call upon reserves of creativity and resilience to live full and loving lives while doing all they can to protect and assist their mentally ill kin. *THE ROOT IS BITTER, THE ROOT IS SWEET In the Shadow of Madness* is for them. May sweetness prevail.

— *Dolores Brandon, New York 2016*
TRACES @www.doloresbrandon.com

Alvin John Brandon

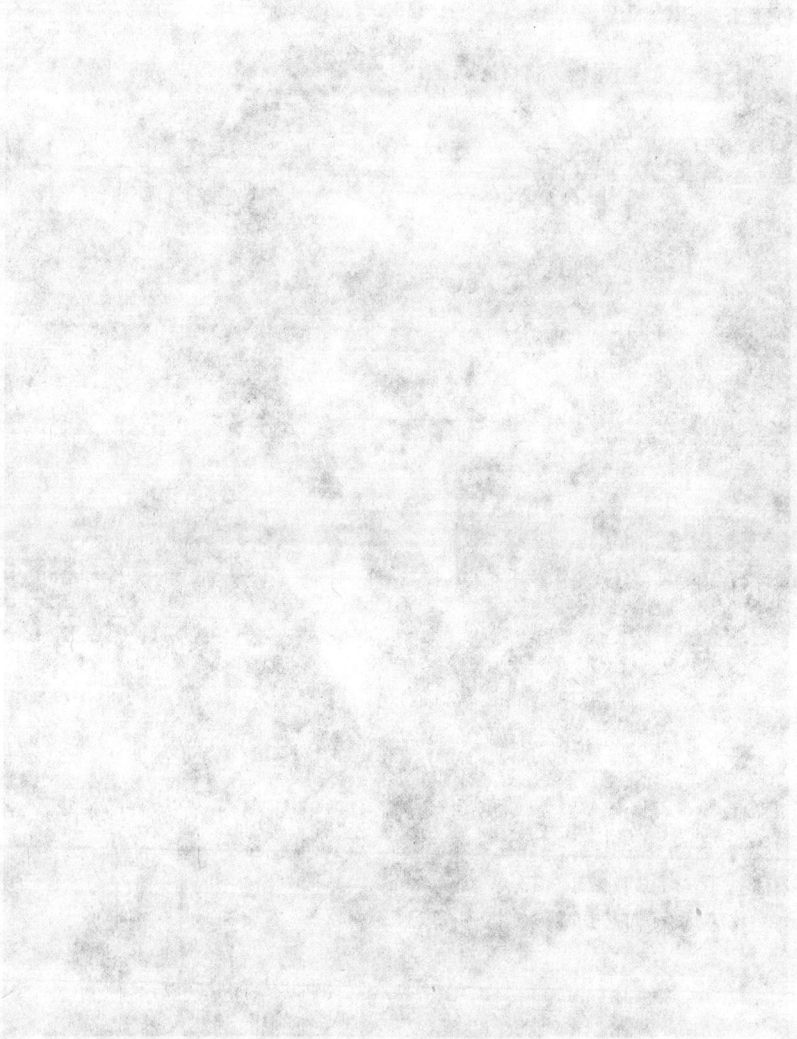

Morning

. . . Many things the gods achieve beyond our judgment. What we thought is not confirmed and what we thought not God contrives. And so it happens in this story.

Medea, Euripides

*F*irst it was Windsor, then
Chatham, Kitchener, Stratford, Collingwood—
a gypsy's trail around and between.
From four years old on it was Toronto.

❖ ❖ ❖ ❖

Chatham 1943

The first child, a late summer's day,
  born at St. Joseph's (St. Joseph, husband to Mary:
Mary Immaculate).

Mum, you tell me I'm exactly what you wanted—
a girl with large dark eyes.
You name me Dolores because you love that name—
Our Lady of Sorrows.
A slip of the tongue, perhaps.
A naming of the underbelly of your own world
fraught with disappointments.
A name profoundly Catholic. A memorial
to the passing of your religious freedom.
A name one invokes in prayer:

        Dolorosa, hear me,
        take away my pain and sorrow
        ease my burden, help me
        bear this cross of marital warfare.

The name a prophesy of what was to come.

*W*hen I was twenty-seven years old, Mum,
I had a vision:
    I go back before the birth. Once inside
    I remember the lights flashing bright,
    the walls of your belly—paper thin,
    your voice—a moist and delicate reed crying:

        Don't do it. I beg you,
        let me go.

Dad, his great frame across you, threatening.
His hands, mighty instruments of rage—
rage at all 'Marys,' all women, all bearers of children.
His voice pulsing pain:

        You'll destroy me. You, your father, the Church
        that controls you, the school system that's fired
        you. How are we to live if everyone rejects us?

It was after this you left him for a while,
left Windsor for "home"—
Mémère and
Pépère's farm on the River Road, Dover.
There you awaited my birth.
There you sang.
Your voice—the most hallowed memory of that time:
    "Ave Maria" in French, "Our Father" in English,
    lullabies embroidered in silver and gold.

I was born on a stream of salty tears,
and the gentle waves of outgoing tides.

Dad's arms formed a cradle of beech.
I felt the quiver of hummingbirds in his hands.

The flood waters rose again only two days later when
I was baptized Catholic against Dad's will.
He turned against my name that day, and
It became my dress of thorns.

6

MORNING

He did his best to hold me close, but
the nectar was no longer as sweet.

Still, I was the reconciliation,
I was the Love,
I was the reason to push on.

*W*hat was known is unknown.
1943 gets to be 1944

Mum sang:
(from Mignon by Ambroise Thomas)
> *Connais-tu le pays où fleurit*
> *l'oranger? Le pays des fruits*
> *d'or et des roses vermeilles,*

I remember responding to
 That song
   That voice
     That tongue.

My eyes say yes, Maman.
That land is you, that
golden fruit, that
vermillion rose.
That land is you
and Daddy.

> *Où la brise est plus douce*
> *et l'oiseau plus léger, Où dans*
> *toute saison butinent les abeilles,*

My gurglings answer
yes, Maman your
breath is the breeze
so tender. Your voice
the flight of the bird.
And Daddy's the honeybee.

Où rayonne et sourit, comme un
bienfait de Dieu, Un Éternel
printemps sous un ciel toujours bleu!

My skin tingles yes,
Maman. Life with you
is eternally Spring.

And Daddy's smile's a
blessing from God.
Your azure eyes—the sky.

Hèlas!

I'll never forget you

Que ne puis-je te suivre Vers ce rivage
heureux d'où le sort m'exila!

I, too, know the river
I am with you in your exile
I share your longings

C'est là! c'est là que je voudrais
vivre, Aimer, aimer et mourir!

I go with you in life
I go with you in love
I go with you in death

C'est là que je voudrais vivre,
c'est là! oui, c'est là!

8

— *1944 continues* —

Kitchener/Waterloo.
Marilyn.
Marilyn was born there in October.
We lived above the Fritzes'.

Little sister. Who are you?
The songs are no longer
only for me and Daddy,
now the songs are for three.

An oral history of those days begins here
as Mum remembers and shares with me
the details of that time of our lives:

> Often, when Marilyn cried,
> the Fritzes would fight under us.
> Dad said, "This is no good. We've got to move."
> But we found people didn't want to rent to
> couples with babies. So, we went to Ma Brandon's,
> in Collingwood, and Dad left me there with you two girls while
> he looked for a place to stay.
> I guess, being his mother, Ma felt obliged to take us in, but I
> didn't feel we were especially welcome.
> At the time she was supporting herself taking in boarders. She'd
> been doing that for years—since the Depression; and at
> mealtimes she'd seat me alone with you and Marilyn at a small
> table separate from the main diners.

Again:
> That song
> > That voice
> > > That tongue.

> *Connais-tu la maison où l'on*
> *m'attend là-bas?*
> *La salle aux lambris d'or, où des hommes*
> *de marbre M'appelent*
> *dans la nuit en me tendant les bras?*

Yes, I know the house, Maman;
the rooms are you and Daddy.
He calls to me in the night,
Maman, and I dream of his embrace.

> *Et la cour où l'on danse*
> *à l'ombre d'un grand arbre?*
> *Et le lac transparent où glissent*
> *sur les eaux Mille bateaux légers*
> *pareils à des oiseaux!*

10

MORNING

Yes, I know the tree, Maman;
the black walnut where you
teach me to walk. And yes,
I know the river, Maman;
behind the house where the
boats glide past. At the sight,
your laughter's sweet as the birds'.

Hèlas!

No, I'll never forget you.

> *que ne puis-je te suivre*
> *Vers ce pays lointain d'où•*
> *le sort m'exila!*

I, too, am in exile,
so far from my home.

> *C'est là, c'est là que je voudrais vivre,*
> *aimer, aimer, et mourir!*
> *C'est là que je voudrais vivre,*
> *c'est là, oui, c'est là!*

I go with you in life
I go with you in love
I go with you in death

> *Oui, c'est là.*

Never do I forget you.

❖ ❖ ❖ ❖

Mum's family homestead on River Road,
Dover, Chatham, Ontario, 1920s.

Mum (Jeanne Julienne) Stratford, Ontario 1940's

Winter 1945

Dad found a place.
We left Ma's.

Mum remembers:
        I couldn't believe that farm he found for us to live!
        Everything froze—the pipes, the toilet, the bottles
        of warm milk I'd make for you two babies. Why
        he chose that desolate place, that mink farm
        outside Kitchener/Waterloo, I'll never know.
        Whatever possessed him to think we'd be happy
        there in winter? And Marilyn, poor child, crying,
        crying out against the cold. I remember pulling
        her crib as close as I could to the coal-fired stove I
        had to load, dividing the blankets between you
        both, and me sleeping with my overcoat on in
        that barn-like room where the drafts swirled
        'round my head.

I imagine Mum praying
        "Sainte Marie, mère de Dieu, priez pour
        nous pécheurs, maintenant, et à l'heure de notre mort.
        Amen."

Resuming our story, she remembers:
        I missed my own mother so. You, Dolores, were
        walking then; you'd follow me outside when I'd be
        hanging diapers. You were a curly-headed
        Shirley Temple, walking proud as a porridge pot,
        steaming through the drifts of snow shoveled high
        by our landlord, Mr. Bristlen. You and Marilyn,
        my two little ones, were all the company I had
        during the week when Alvin was away working.

Alvin was Dad's name.
        He was manager then at the Singer Sewing
        Machine Store in Stratford.

13

I understand why
that life was so hard for Mum.
After all, life before Dad had been
so different. The homestead
there on the River Road, Dover
was so very beautiful. On that
soil—so rich and fertile—
Pépère grew tobacco, tomatoes,
sugar beets and corn. They
had an orchard of peach, pear,
apple and cherry. Beauty and plenty
were everyday things.

The marriage became a kind of exile:
There would be so many losses.

❖ ❖ ❖ ❖

Spring 1945

We moved to Stratford.
Mum sang—
     Delilah
          (from *Samson & Delilah* by Saint Saens):

          Printemps qui commence. Portant
          l'espérance Aux cœurs amoureux,

That song
     That voice
          That tongue.

          Ton souffle qui passe De la terre
          efface Les jours malheureux.

Washes sorrow from the heart

          Tout brûle en notre âme, Et ta douce
          flamme Vient sécher nos pleurs;

Gives permission to desire

          Tu rends à la terre, Par un doux
          mystère, Les fruits, et les fleurs.

Is forever the fruit, forever
the flower, forever the
mysterious yearning.

          En vain je suis belle!

Is its beauty a dream?

          Mon cœur plein d'amour, Pleurant
          l'infidèle, Attend son retour!
          Vivant d'espérance, Mon cœur
          désolé Garde souvenance Du
          bonheur passé!

Maman, with a heart so in love
with a man your Papa so reviled,
did your despair disappear
in the happiness we knew?
Never a direct answer to this question.
Only . . .

> Stratford was very pretty that spring and summer.
> We were living in a big brick house with people
> named Beatle. You couldn't say that word very
> well, and so called them the "Beeo's." You were
> not quite two. Anyway, every morning you'd run
> to get the milk left at the front door. You'd take a
> bottle in your arms, carry it to the bottom of the
> stairs, and call, "Mrs. Beeeooo," so loud and clear;
> she loved playing that little game with you each
> day.

*T*hrough this oral history
dialogue we bond anew;
I love to hear
these family stories.

It's as if I'm a child
again, resting safely
in my mother's arms.

> That house was on a lot that sloped down toward
> the Avon River. One day I left you alone in your
> playpen while I was inside doing some chores;
> somehow you got out and walked down to the
> shore where the swans would paddle by. You used
> to like calling to the swans, and together we'd
> often toss breadcrumbs their way. That day, it
> seems, you were wading right into the water
> when some people happened to notice and catch
> you before you'd gone too far. They brought you
> to the house.

I got such a fright when I saw you soaking wet
and crying. I could hardly believe what they told
me had happened. I called Dad at the store. He
came rushing home. The thought that we could
lose you was more than we could bear.

That song
    That voice
        That tongue.

> *À la nuit tombante J'irai triste amante,*
> *M'asseoir au torrent, L'attendre en*
> *pleurant Chassant ma tristesse,*
> *S'il revient un jour, À lui ma tendresse,*
> *Et la douce ivresse, Qu'un brûlant*
> *amour Garde à son retour!*

I remember:
When night falls
a sadness blackens
the day.
I lie outside and
hear crying. Maman,
why does your tenderness
scorch him?
Why does Dad's passion
leave burns?

> *Chassant ma tristesse, S'il revient un*
> *jour, À lui ma tendresse Et la douce*
> *ivresse Qu'un brûlant amour Garde*
> *à son retour!*

I go with you in life
I go with you in love
I go with you in death

*D*idn't you go away
that autumn, Maman?

> Yes, that year the government decided to give
> teachers a special bonus if they'd been teaching
> five years. We really needed the money, and since
> I'd put in four years before they fired me,
> I thought if I were to get a job in the public school
> system for a year, I could get my permanent
> teacher's certificate, and collect the money I felt
> was due me.

It was a cruel
system that fired
Mum then:

> She went to the School Board
> Chairman (in Nov. '42) to say
> she'd be getting married.
> She doesn't remember the Chairman's
> name, and doesn't want to.
> He asked her, "To whom?"
> She answered, "Alvin Brandon."
> Hearing the name, Brandon,
> he suspected Dad wasn't French,
> and asked, "Where's he from?"
> She said, "Collingwood."
> (It happens to be well-known Orangeman
> —hence Anglo-Irish Protestant—country.)
> His face disapproved as he asked,
> "Is he Catholic?"
> She said no.
> He advised her:

> > *You'd be better*
> > *to forget him. Believe me,*
> > *the marriage won't work.*
> > *And you won't be allowed to teach*
> > *with us here in the Windsor*
> > *Separate School System, if you do.*

Despite his warning,
they married that Friday.
On Monday, she was fired.

Mum remembers:

>Two little girls, students of mine, came to the
house with flowers that afternoon. "We're going
to miss you, Mlle. Gagner," they whispered
sweetly.

She resumes the story
she started to tell earlier:

>So, I looked in the paper and got a job in
Curryville, a town not that far away, but too far
for Dad to travel every day. It meant I had to be
away from home during the week. Dad would
drive me up on Monday morning, and pick me up
Friday afternoon. Imagine the nerve of me leaving
you children. Just thinking about it now really
shakes me up. We hired a woman to help Dad
while I was gone. Her name was Margaret.
She was very nice, and took good care of you. She had
her own little girl with her, Marlene, who was six.
Margaret had recently divorced her husband. And,
although we didn't know it when we hired her, she
was pregnant. When we found out, we kept her
anyway, and everything worked out. She had her
baby at Easter when I was home for the holiday
week. Then because Margaret needed a rest
Ma came to help out for a while. I think Margaret
gave her baby away.

❖ ❖ ❖ ❖

— 1946 —

While I was away in Curryville, Dad invented "the baby-minder." Marilyn wasn't quite one, and you were just two. You were both very active and Dad worried that you might fall out of your high-chairs. So he created a kind of stirrup that he attached to the tray of the highchair and looped around your ankles to prevent you from standing and possibly falling. It was really quite something. He sewed them himself when he had free time at

the Singer store. Customers there liked them and started to place orders. Naturally he got very excited. He even took out a patent on it in Canada, the United States and Great Britain.

Then, some local furniture stores agreed to stock them.

Singer, however, wasn't too happy with his sideline and told him he'd have to choose. He chose the baby-minder, deciding to sink every-thing we had into the business that summer. He took my last month's paycheck and bought a used house-trailer so we could live and travel through-out Ontario and Quebec selling the baby-minders. By then he had a manufacturer. He even had a tag made up (in English and French) with a photo-graph of Marilyn seated in the highchair, baby-minder in place.

I remember that picture:
   Marilyn—golden girl
   starlit eyes of blue—
   soft curls of strawberry
   blonde tumbling 'round
   your cupid's face.

That picture stayed in my mind.
I wondered secretly, why
isn't it me?
Does Daddy still love
me, too?

> We sold everything we had, which wasn't much.
> I'd just bought a beautiful new bedroom set, my
> first, and there I was standing up in that trailer,
> my arms outstretched to prevent the dresser from
> rolling inward as we delivered it to its new owner!

I imagine Dad saying:
> So the road is our home
> this summer. Come along
> my dear ones, climb into
> the old Nash; see how it
> pulls the trailer! We'll
> head on up through Niagara,
> and the Caledon Hills, on
> along the St. Lawrence, and
> into the little towns of
> Quebec where your mother
> can talk for us in French.
> Wave goodbye to the Beatles,
> now. You'll see, I'll be a rich man
> yet. You girls are my
> treasure trove. We'll cook
> our food in the open air
> as the sun rises and sets
> each day. We'll live like
> gypsies, my barefoot love.
> See, I remembered to pack
> your Hawaiian guitar. So
> wipe those tears aside; play
> "Eyes of Blue" for me, and I'll
> tell you what we're going to do.

Singer Sewing Machine Store where Dad was manager,
Stratford, Ontario, 1945.

Dad demonstrating one of the Airway vacuum
cleaners he was selling door-to-door, 1947.

No doubt Mum said:
        Not now. Let's drive. It looks like rain to me.

I imagine:
    The trailer
    makeshift
    hand hewn
    fragile
    the family
    now calling it home.

    An impulse
    to build something
    holds mummy,
    daddy and little
    ones together.

I imagine Dad saying:
        I tell you all I need in
        every town's a good street
        map and a telephone book.
        You'll see, we'll hit all
        the main furniture stores.
        What do you bet? I say
        everyone'll buy a dozen
        at least, maybe two! The
        big stores will use our ad;
        it's complete, picture and
        copy. All they have to do is
        run it for the orders to come
        rolling in. If the stores need
        more stock, they can order
        direct from the factory.
        We'll be on to the next town;
        the baby-minders will be
        selling themselves. Bingo!
        I feel it. We'll be in the money
        faster than you think.

I remember:
    Highways, and byways,
    towns, and cities.
    Stopping, and starting,
    the car overheating, stinking.
    Babies we were—vomiting
    into paper bags, shitting
    and peeing in bushes on
    back roads.

I can still hear
Mum saying:
    Pull down your panties;
    hold them like this, see;
    they won't get wet, or dirty.

She laughs as she
tells me this story:
    Oh, the things you do when you're twenty-five!
    We were outside Hamilton one night; it wasn't always easy to
    find a place to park, but we'd pulled into a low-lying wooded
    area along the highway. No sooner did the sun go down than
    mosquitoes swarmed up around us like a cloud out of nowhere.
    I grabbed whatever coverings I could lay my hands on—sheets,
    towels, anything to throw over you girls, and we were out of
    there as fast as we could go. Oh, boy. I can laugh about it now,
    but it wasn't funny then. We ended up in a service station
    parking lot that night. Oh, gull!

Not all the grounds had good facilities.
  Some had showers, most didn't.
It wasn't easy to keep clean,
I tell you!

We had a Coleman stove and a pressure cooker,
but never cooked in the trailer; we did all that
outside. We weren't risking having a fire in there.
During the day Dad would go into the towns
to sell the baby-minders, and I'd stay at the camp-
grounds with you.

I remember playing:
Pat-a-cake, pat-a-cake,
baker's man. Bake me a
cake as fast as you can.
Pat it and prick it, and
mark it with B. And put
it in the oven for baby and
me. For baby and me, for
baby and me. And there
will be plenty for baby
and me.

A lot of gypsies lived in these places. We didn't mingle with them, though. People warned us, saying they'd steal. We never really had any trouble, but I remembered how when I was a girl they used to pass by in covered wagons, drawn by thin mules, sometimes horses, and inside the wagons they'd have a pack of dogs. My mother would say, "Don't go near the road when those gypsies pass by."

Ah, well. You were happy there, I think—playing outside all day. At night you'd fall asleep without a peep.

I think of "The Riddle Song":
I gave my love a cherry that has no stone.
I gave my love a chicken that has no bone.
I gave my love a ring that has no end.
I gave my love a baby with no cryin'.

How can there be a cherry that has no stone?
How can there be a chicken that has no bone?
How can there be a ring that has no end?
How can there be a baby with no cryin'?

A cherry when it's bloomin' it has no stone.
A chicken when it's pippin' it has no bone.
A ring when it's rollin' it has no end.
A baby when it's sleepin' there's no cryin'.

25

I ask Mum:
>   Nights were not always so tender;
>   when did the violence begin?

Without hesitation,
she answers:
>   It was very bad one night in the trailer.

I imagine:
>   Mum sobbing as she climbs
>   into the bunk next to him.
>   Her words might have been:

>   *Hold me close my darling; I'm*
>   *so afraid. Take me in your*
>   *arms, your great arms. I*
>   *fell in love with your smile.*
>   *But . . . I don't know how long*
>   *I have for this dream. It's too*
>   *hard. We need a real home.*

Perhaps:
he hears her words,
and the pain of her fears,
but the cries pinch a nerve
in his hands. So, he closes his
rage 'round her throat in
response to an old troll
in his head.

I relive the scene:
She begs him:
>   *Let go.*

Then whimpers:
>   *I can't breathe.*

There's a blow to the head.
And we children wake in
the bunk up above, where
everything's shaking.

He pulls away like a boxer
preparing the next blow.
A tongue-lashing ensues:

> *You cunt, you bitch,*
> *you ball-breaker you!*

I probe to know more:
　　Why did you stay?

　　　　I don't know, I loved him. It wasn't his fault.

And more:
　　That wasn't the only time, was it?
　　It happened a lot?

　　　　He was trying so hard. He wanted the best for you
　　　　girls and me. But there weren't any reorders for
　　　　the baby-minders coming in. Some people said it
　　　　was barbaric to have a child's feet tied up. Dad was
　　　　so hurt when he heard them say that—he cried.

Again, I remember
　　Her song
　　　　Her voice
　　　　　　Her tongue
　　　　　　　　A fragment
　　　　　　　　　　(Micaela's song from "Carmen"):

> *Je dis, que rien ne m'épouvante*
> *Je dis, hélas! que je réponds de moi;*
> *Mais j'ai beau faire la vaillante, Au fond du*
> *cœur je meurs d'effroi! Seule en ce lieu*
> *sauvage,*
> *Toute seule j'ai peur, mais j'ai tort d'avoir*
> *peur; Vous me donnerez du courage,*
> *Vous me protègerez, Seigneur!*

　　　　This love had a
　　　　hurricane face.
　　　　The trailer stood—

its windows cracked,
its sashes torn,
the roof leaking
over the beds.

The sun shone autumn soon.

I want to know everything I can, so I ask:
Mum, where did
we go from there?
> We put you girls in foster care near Stratford.
> *Oh my God.*

She cries as she recalls
the event.
> I never told you this story before.

I say:
I remember somehow.
> I don't know how you could. We never, ever
> talked about it in front of you.

I insist:
But I remember.
Tell me, how did it happen?

> Dad wanted to settle in Toronto. He felt he could get a
> job there. We still had the trailer, though, and there was
> nowhere to park it. We thought of going to Chatham,
> but my father wouldn't let us leave it on the farm, so we
> went back to Stratford. Pépère was fed up with Dad; he
> wanted me to divorce him, but I wouldn't. Sometimes I
> think maybe I should have. But I'd been taught
> marriage is forever. And I loved your Dad so much.
> He didn't love me though, certainly not the way I
> loved him. He never did, and he told me so.

I know what she says is true:
until his dying day, Dad wouldn't
admit that he loved her.
I know she never deserved that.

It was a marriage that should never have been.
But it was and somehow they endured;
somehow they prospered and a life was built.
A life that had its bitterness
and its sweetness always
mixed.

I recall hardly a
minute in which the two
were not fully intertwined.

*M*um continues the oral history:

> Anyway, we needed time to get settled in
> Toronto, and we both had to find jobs. But who
> was to look after you girls? Dad knew the
> manager of the Children's Aid Society in Stratford,
> so he went to him for advice. He told Dad there
> was a nice family in Blight who'd take care of you
> for awhile. And that's what happened.

> Dad and I went to Toronto. I got a job at a children's
> clothing store on St. Clair. Dad started selling Airway
> vacuum cleaners door-to-door. We rented a room on Nairn
> Street. On weekends we'd visit you girls.

Her voice quivers as
she tells this story.

> One day, I'll never forget. We were about to leave;
> the Blights had you, each one in their arms. They
> were good people, kind, really. You were laugh-
> ing, happy. As we were getting ready to go Mrs.
> Blight said to me, "I don't know how you can bear to leave
> two such lovely children." My heart
> broke. I wanted to scream. How could she think
> I *wanted* to leave you? During the week, I missed
> you so. I was crying all the time.

> Not long after that Dad said, "That's it, we're
> going to get them." And we did. I quit that job,

and we packed up again—you girls and I—and
went to Ma's in Collingwood while Dad stayed with Aunt
Margaret and her family in Toronto.

Aunt Margaret's
one of Dad's younger sisters.
(She married Hubert Lee).

Then in November I got a call from Chatham.
Mémère and Aunt Julienne had been in an accident.

Aunt Julienne is
Mum's younger sister.

They were coming home from a wedding. Jul was driving.
Both were hurt. Mémère had a broken leg, and Jul, a
concussion. They wondered if I could come to help. Well,
of course I could, so we moved there. Dad would come on
weekends, and I'd take you to Toronto by train sometimes.
You girls loved that ride. Oh, my! We'd all be at Aunt
Margaret's! In that narrow two-storey they had on
McRoberts Street.

There were only three small bedrooms, so we were a
houseful—Aunt Margaret, Uncle Hubert, and their three
children. You'd all have such a good time playing. Oh, my.
We were there for Christmas that year. In Chatham, as well,
you had fun with your cousins—Glorianna had just the four
children then.

Glorianna's my godmother,
Mum's older sister (married to
Norman Bélanger; they had nine
children in all over the years).

Remember they were living in the bungalow, near
the road, on the other side of the barn at Pépère's?
Anyway, everything was nice. Everyone was good to us.

30

I remember Pépère's that winter:

> The slippery feel of stocking
> feet sliding 'long grey enamel
> painted stairs winding from
> kitchen to cellar. The heady
> smell of gas, invisible vapors
> lingering 'round summer stove
> now closed. A labyrinth of
> basement rooms, cool cement
> floors, corrugated tin wash tubs,
> laundry sinks, storage spaces,
> closets: a perfect place for
> hide-and-seek. Learning to foxtrot,
> dancing on Pépère's toes. Laughter
> rippling 'gainst thin pine doors.
> Daydreams drifting as snow-white light
> winked in through frost-built castles
> and ice-carved butterfly wings on
> window panes in February.

> French was spoken there (except when
> Daddy came. Mum says he felt rejected
> when they didn't speak English).
> Mum's voice in French—
> was it louder, gayer, freer?

>> We were in Chatham 'til spring. Then Dad bought
>> the house at Long Branch. It cost $2600. My
>> goodness, you couldn't buy a thing for that price
>> today. He made all that money in one month,
>> selling vacuum cleaners.

Was that the year he
won a gold watch and
a trip to Toledo?

>> I'm not sure. Maybe. He was always winning
>> prizes in those days. He was a fantastic salesman,
>> tops! Those Airways were selling for $75, and he'd

get a $25 commission on each one, so he had to
have sold over a hundred of them in one month!

I went to Toronto soon after so he could show
me our new home. It was a cottage really, right
on the beach, a street called Lake Promenade. At
that time a small community of cottagers lived
there at the Lakeshore; most stayed only for the
summers so many of the homes were boarded up,
but a few people were there year 'round.

Today, all of that's gone. It's now Marie Curtis
Park.

Anyway, there was the cottage, white with blue
trim, sitting up on four posts, facing Lake
Ontario. When I saw it, I cried. I cried and I cried.
I thought, oh no how can we live here? There was
no running water, no indoor toilet, only two
rooms. Thank goodness there was electricity.

How did Dad react to
you crying like that?

He felt bad, I guess, because on our way back to
Aunt Margaret's we stopped at a hotel there near Dundas and
Highway 27 for a beer. He thought that might be a bit of a treat,
might cheer me up.

After all, he explained, we did need a place where we could all
be together. He didn't like us living apart. And finding a place
wasn't easy. It was the same old story wherever we'd go—no
one wanted to rent to you if you had children! Aunt Margaret
used to say, "Landlords don't want people for tenants, they
want birds who'll just fly in and out."

We'd laugh about it, really.

Dad, Mum, Dolores and Marilyn,
Long Branch, 1947.

The cottage on the shores of Lake Ontario,
Long Branch, 1947.

I made myself accept the cottage.
Dad and I used the bigger of the two rooms for
our bedroom, and gave you girls the smaller room.
That meant our room served as kitchen, living
room, bedroom. There was a large old wood-
burning stove in there. We had to carry our water
in pails from a city well across the street.
Sometimes I'd go along the beach picking up
sticks to use in the stove for cooking. It was
pretty primitive living, I tell you. Eventually,
we did get a hot-plate.

Once we got settled, we did have some good times
there. Mrs. Smart, the woman who sold the place
to us, left behind an old piano. It wasn't a very
good one; the back was made of wood instead of
steel, so it didn't stay in tune too well. But, you
know Dad, he loved to play and sing. He had
a good sense of pitch, too, and liked to fix things, so
he'd sort of tune it up as necessary. At the time
there were two other families living nearby; they'd
come over on weekends, or in the evenings. One
of the men, a Mr. Carter, played guitar. Dad and
he'd get together and we'd have a sing-song.

I remember:
> *On top of Old Smokey,*
> *All covered with snow,*
> *I lost my true lover,*
> *A courtin' too slow.*

That song over the years became
a theme song of sorts for Dad.
He'd sing it in an exaggerated
cowboy style, in a key of mock
pathos, a hound dog quality
haunting the tone. As Marilyn
and I grew older and put on
our own performances, we'd
imitate him singing that song.

Becoming him, so-to-speak, I think
I learned to feel the unshed tears
that lay in his heart.

> *A courtin's a pleasure,*
> *A partin' is grief,*
> *A false-hearted lover,*
> *Is worse than a thief.*

Years later, after he'd suffered
several serious mental breakdowns,
I found a packet of Dad's handwritten
ravings in a dresser drawer.
In them he addressed a girl, a
sweetheart he'd loved and lost.
He alluded to her beauty; recalled
a red dress she sometimes wore.

> *A thief he will rob you,*
> *And take what you have,*
> *But a false hearted lover,*
> *Sends you to your grave.*

Meanwhile,
Mum recalls:

> In summer the beach at Long Branch was lovely.
> We'd go swimming. Dad bought a small motor
> boat, and we'd go for long rides on the lake.
> Sometimes Aunt Margaret and her family would
> come over; they'd bring a lunch and stay all day.
> We'd have great fun, you children swimming,
> building sand castles while we talked and laughed.
> On weekends some of Dad's coworkers might drop
> by. We'd sing and dance all night. That cottage
> would rock!

> The one bad thing there in the summer were the
> frogs. They'd croak all night, and Dad was one
> who couldn't stand any noise while sleeping. Me, I
> can sleep through anything, but not him; he'd be

36

up throwing stones into the marsh at the side of
the house. I think he even had a BB gun.

> *They'll hug you and kiss you,*
> *And tell you more lies,*
> *Than the spikes in a railroad,*
> *Or stars in the skies.*

The winter wasn't exactly pleasant. It was pretty
cold and the cottage wasn't insulated. We did have
a Quebec heater, though, and I think we got some
coal for the stove. But Dad caught a really bad
cold, almost like pneumonia. He was in bed quite
awhile. That meant he wasn't making any money.
As a salesman, he was on straight commission.
Mind you, he liked to work that way, and he was
forever selling something, even before I knew him.
It was in his blood, I guess. But it was stressful,
and dry spells made him very anxious.

9 begin to know two aspects
of God—Creator and
Destroyer—because I know
my Daddy, and God's
in every man.

His (psych)les parallel
the seasons.
In summer he's a day at the beach,
a sand castle:
fragile, magical—
a boat afloat—
an occasional squall in the night.

In winter, the beach lies barren
the sand castle broken,
its tunnels hollow,
the boat ashore and lonely.

37

Mum remembers:

       One morning that spring there was a torrential
downpour, water flooded into the cottage. Dad
was at work, so I was alone there with you girls. I
put you both up on the bed away from the rising
water, put Dad's hip boots on thinking I'd wade
across the road for help. I was just about to step
out when I heard a man frantically hollering,
"Don't walk there, get back inside." It was Mr.
Ward, an employee of the water filtration plant
across the road. "Stay where you are, I'll come and
get you," he yelled. I threw together a few
things—clothes, I suppose.
       Shortly after, Mr. Ward arrived at the beach side
of the house in a small boat to rescue us. He said,
"You could have drowned, lost your life if you'd
stepped into that water." When I think of it now,
I shudder. The water was flowing so swiftly! In
fact, during Hurricane Hazel, a lot of those
cottages, including ours, were washed entirely
away.

(Hurricane Hazel
would hit Toronto
in 1954.)

       Mr. Ward took us to a nearby house safely sit-
uated on a hill. From there I called Dad. He took
us to Aunt Margaret's where we stayed for a day
or two waiting for the water to subside. What a
mess we found when we returned. Sediment every-
where. We cleaned it up and moved back in,
but found ourselves almost afraid to go to sleep at
night for worry. So, we put the place up for sale,
and Dad immediately started looking for a new
place to live.

Disheveled white frame cottage
on stilts like an aging sea gull;
cool in the shade of overhanging trees
observing cold grey stretch of
sky hanging across Lake Ontario.

MORNING

We were sojourners again,
adrift on the rising tides.

My sad heart is aching,
I'm weary today,
My lover has left me,
I'm feelin' this way.

Moving was a way of life.
There had been ten moves in my first five years.
There would be five more before I was ten.

Summer 1948
— Indian Road —

A second floor walk-up.

I remember:
  coming in through the front door, a door we shared with people
  living on the first floor, Russian immigrants who boiled cabbage
  in vinegar and garlic every day.

I liked climbing the steep enclosed staircase, though dank and
dingy, liked the feel of the worn wood railing against my hand; it
led to our door, the door I opened into the kitchen filled with
sunlight.

Mum, do you remember the day Aunt Julienne came up those
steps with that live duck she brought for dinner? Do you
remember you and her laughing; your voices melodious and
sweet in summer as Christmas carols?

Mum, you were only twenty-eight then. So young. I wish I'd
been able to know you as you were then. That is, know you
more deeply, more equally, more like a confidante than a girl
knows her mother.

Was the day Aunt Julienne came with the duck as much fun for
you as it seemed to me? You had a way of enjoying simple
things like that—a joy, a gaiety in response to life's everydayness.
You know, I don't ever remember seeing you bored, never even
once saying you were; you always gave yourself over so wholly
to the necessity of the moment.

Like the way you hand-fed Dad when he had that bad case of
mumps. (We all had them at once—Marilyn, he and I—in the
dead of winter when everything felt so cramped and dark, the
little rooms crowding in upon us, the piano closed and silent so
as not to bother the man downstairs who wore a black fedora at
all times and worked at home, said he was a reporter—for whom
we'd never know . . .)

40

MORNING

There was Dad wrapped in a robe and woolen blankets; his
cheeks swollen pouches, his neck a column of throbbing pain,
tears falling from his eyes, poor thing, picturing, perhaps, the
twenty-seven years his own mother spoon-fed Clara, his older
sister—she suffering an infantile paralysis for which there was no
known cure.

I believe he carried Clara's image with him always—like an egg,
an emblem of life's fragility.

Mum, you were his mother then.

That spring Dad bought himself a dazzling new maroon Monarch
coupe, and drove south to Miami with "Uncle Rosaire." They danced
in Havana, returned home with watermelons and coconuts and tales
of Georgia fields where Negro workers sang.

He planned to have us move, to own an orange grove, soak up the sun
among the cockatoos. He was a dreamer, a vagabond; a high wire
trapeze artist lived in his soul. It didn't happen, though. U.S.
Immigration wouldn't allow in a man who'd suffered a mental
breakdown in the army at twenty-five.

No matter.

The street in front of our house was always bustling—women and
children—hopscotch, double dutch, and talk of what was for lunch.
Amid the chatter and giggles of young girls I caught myself admiring
the beautiful teardrop breasts of one—as she bent over, I glimpsed
past her crimson neckline into a dream of future desire.

Mum, remember the day Marilyn and her friend pee'd outside,
against the wall of the house next door? You might never have known
had I not told. You were so mad, and I was eager to see
Marilyn punished. You made her wash it away with a pail of hot
water. The neighbors watched. She hated me for telling. I didn't
care.

Recently Marilyn told me she remembers only the
delight she felt in peeing there.

41

Dolores (left) and Marilyn (right), 1948.

MORNING

Mum, you dressed us like dolls, twin angels.
    At night you'd wash our hair,
    twist it in rags for ringlets.
    Every day we'd wear a new ribbon.
    Then—my first haircut:
            it's a loss of who I think I am.
            I don't want anyone to see me.
            I hide behind your skirt as we walk home.
            I feel only half of what I was
            before they cut it.

Did I still have the longest eyelashes, the biggest eyes? Would
older girls still ask to borrow them for an evening out with a
boy? Something was gone, and I didn't know where it went, or
exactly what it was.

That year I remember telling you, "I don't want to dress like
Marilyn any more." She was in kindergarten (Fern Avenue
School) then. For me kindergarten was a paper snowflake—
crumpled, lost and tossed.

And Grade One's now only a first day memory: schoolmate's
stories of witch teacher mean; me screaming fear crying,
"Mother, Mother, never leave me." "You must," the principal
ordered, and walked me in.

The teacher gently tossed a little bouncing ball, and I agreed to
play.

❖ ❖ ❖ ❖

43

Fall 1949
Denton Avenue

Scarborough: a modest neighborhood on Toronto's east end.
Not what you'd call fashionable. A little seedy, a little neglected.
Working class affordable.

The house:
    A single family detached odd thing. Set so the basement was
above ground, the first floor was thrust up higher than houses
nearby. It wore a sheath of common asphalt brick. The front
door was off to the right. The yard was a humble little patch of
land. The driveway, an afterthought at the foot.

    We moved there as autumn turned to winter—November.
School was stopped, started anew.

First day of school:
    Mum took us by the hands. We walked silently for a block or
two along Denton. Apprehension mounted as we turned the
corner onto Danforth Avenue—the street our new school was
named after. It was a bleak walk, few trees; those trees that
were, were bare of leaves. The sidewalk was shabby, broken,
under construction. Trucks passed their fumes without shame.
No sun shone.

    That school's a close-up view (now): a door opens into the
classroom to which I am assigned. A woman fills the (memory)
frame. Her curly grey hair is radiant against a warm white light.
I whisper so only Mum hears, "Isn't she pretty?" A wave of
relief passes through Mum's arm; with a smile she lets go my
hand. Miss Laidlaw gracefully walks me in.

— *Winter* —

Danforth Avenue revealed a pleasure or two. Piano playing,
children's voices, laughter, drew me to a barn-like building I
passed by each day. At the door, left open, I relaxed in the warm air
that escaped and watched girls my age learn to dance tap, twirl
batons, cartwheel and somersault. I wanted to be in there too. But
Dad said no, and once he said that there was no negotiating, no
reversing his decision. He said something about "the silly costumes
they wear." Frilly blue, white, pink tutus with silver sequins and
plastic tiaras—why, I thought they were awfully pretty.

Again, Mum and I resume
the oral history dialogue:
> That year Dad was having a hard time sleeping.
> He decided to take on an extra job—driving a truck. What
> happened was: by chance one day we were out driving
> and I noticed a lot of trucks parked in a yard with the
> name THIBODEAU in big bold letters. We stopped, and
> sure enough it was Roy Thibodeau. Roy was a school
> chum of mine, his family was from Chatham, Windsor.
> And here he was in Toronto; this was his business. Dad
> decided maybe Roy would give him a job. We went back
> a few days later and asked. Roy was surprised, couldn't
> believe a man of Dad's quality would want to drive a
> truck. He said, "My good-ness, Jeanne, why would Alvin
> want to do this?
> He's so refined, looks like a doctor, an intellectual,
> professional, I don't understand." I explained Dad was
> having trouble sleeping, thought he could wear himself
> out driving, and maybe sleep. Roy said, "Fine."

In retrospect, it's clear the
sleeplessness was one
symptom of the manic-depressive
illness that was slowly to coil its way
through every aspect of our lives.

> The pay was low. Dad used to put what Roy paid
> him in a jar in a kitchen cupboard. He didn't really

45

need it. Months later when we were packing to
move, again, he found it; we laughed to see how
little it actually was.

— *Spring* —

A business opportunity appeared for Marilyn and me in a magazine ad.
It invited us to order seeds through the mail, sell them, and make a small
profit—a nickel on each package sold. We complied, filling out the
coupon, requesting the catalogue from which we'd choose our stock.
Not long after, the catalogue arrived. It was beautiful, its glossy pages
crowded with yellow sunflowers, purple zinnias, black-eyed susans,
orange marigolds, red rhubarb, rosy tomatoes, sugar snap peas and
more.

The process was so simple: write up the order, send it in and wait for the
mailman to deliver. We did. Little square boxes came, with maybe a
hundred individual packets. We enjoyed feeling the seeds through the
silken paper wrapping. Some were whisper small, almost not there.
Others were so fat and crunchy they'd poke through if we weren't
careful, and Dad warned, "No one'll want a broken bag." We handled
them as gently as we could, though we couldn't ever fully resist shaking
and smelling the packets. We read the names over and over like rhymes
as we arranged them and rearranged them, before finally selling them
door-to-door faster than we ever dreamt, proving we were, after all, our
father's girls.

— *Summer* —

"*Annie Get Your Gun*" was the big movie (the first one I actually
remember seeing). Once home, always ready to play-act, Marilyn and I
decided our four-wheeled wooden wagon made quite a good horse.
We'd take turns being Annie, who got to ride the "horse," and the
cowboy. We'd gallop swiftly from the front of our house, around the
corner and come to a halt in the driveway (stable). We'd kiss goodbye
like movie lovers.

With her golden curls, and sober blue eyes, Marilyn pretended she was
Gabby Hayes. Tucking her hands into her cotton overalls, she walked

fat and silly just like he did. We laughed together, and were each other's true best friend. We'd be there to hold onto as the shadows did fall.

We gathered flowers in Mrs. Elvins' garden next door. Hers—a crazy quilt of pink hollyhocks, white flox and rambling red roses—was better than ours. Often, her kitchen was a nestling place, her living room a radio play—Amos and Andy—where she sat in a rocking chair and we squatted by her knees, listening.

— *Fall again* —

Second grade. Teacher, Miss Brooks. It was the first time I got to be teacher's pet. Sitting close, running errands, I was in paradise. I loved learning script, and became the best writer in class.

My girlfriend and I spent recess laughing, talking, running from boys who wanted a kiss. I told her about the "pouter's bench," a place Dad said "lies over the tracks behind the hill at the back of the school; they put people there who cry too much." I knew he was a tease, but I half believed, and enjoyed testing the tale out on her. The bell rang before I had to prove it was really true.

One week as the weather turned blustery my friend got to stay in at recess because her mother wrote a note requesting permission to do so. I wanted to stay inside, too, but knowing my mother'd never lie on my behalf, I decided to write a note for myself. After all, I thought, "I'm such a good writer—who'll know the difference!"

And so:
> *Dear Miss Brooks:*
> *Please let Dolores stay in at recess.*
> *She seems to be coming down with a cold.*
> *Thank you,*
> *Mrs. Jeanne Brandon*

The note, a folded lie, ached in the heart of Miss Brooks. She couldn't believe I'd do it. I said I didn't. She knew I did. Over. Gone. The hall to detention felt like rain, a cloudburst, a hole in the wall.

47

Mum is pregnant.
She's expecting a baby in March.

One night Dad's a dark shadow stalking.
Early warning signals rumble through the floor.
We sisters awake to Mum crying, screaming.
Struggle, crashing.
Oh no! What's that?
Splintering shards of glass fall like tears
He's slammed her
head and shoulders through the window.
Mummy, Daddy, no!
I wail out against his might.
No, no, no!
But nothing was to thwart his aggression.
Not Mum, not me, not the night.
My cries are a signal he's not bound to obey.
He shakes me silent by the hair.
Why does he beat her so?
Didn't ask. Don't know.
Eyes full of tears, lips pursed 'round pain.

Not long after, Mum went to the hospital.
A few days later she arrived home with
our new baby sister bundled in a blanket,
a baby so plump and sweet we all wanted to eat her.

Dad had hopes for a boy, but it was okay.
After the mumps he'd worried about his potency.
This baby girl was his assurance. He was very happy.
He loved her. She'd be his favorite.
No one else mattered anymore.

Suzanne Julienne Kathleen—that's the name
we gave her.

I begged for the name Kathleen, and
Mum added it onto the registration.

48

If Sue'd been a boy, she'd have been called
Christopher John, after grandfather Brandon,
the ship carpenter
we never knew (he died before Dad married).
The ship carpenter some say was violent,
the man Dad never, ever spoke of.

I thought, "I'm a mother now."
One evening we children were at Mrs. Elvins'. She was our baby-
sitter whenever Mum and Dad went out. Jack, her bloated
boarder, was there; he dared to enter the sacred circle I'd
imagined as a protection 'round Suzanne's cradle. Like a ferocious
mother bird I screeched, "Don't touch, get away!" He laughed,
teased me and didn't move! I hauled off and kicked him good in t
he shins. He got mad, rolled a cigarette, poured a drink, seething
"You're bad." We stared a standoff 'til Mum and Dad came home.
They heard the tale and took his side: "Your behavior's an
embarrassment," they scolded. "Now go on to bed."

A fight for survival was now alive in my bones.

Soon after we moved—before the school year was through.

Dad, Suzanne, Mum, Marilyn, Dolores
Caledonia Road, Toronto,
Ontario, 1951.

Spring 1951
— Caledonia Road —

The house, a tiny brown asphalt bungalow with porch, ivory
painted, low to the ground.

The school, Hughes, not far, up the block and over a bit.
Spring term second grade—third school.

Afraid to say goodbye, hello.
Eyes turned inward.
(They'd need glasses soon.)
Uprooted, lost, friends never to be seen again.

> *Why are we here?*
> *All this moving has me sick.*
> *I'm dizzy now.*
> *Somebody see me, hold me, tell me what to say.*
> *Running, moving,*
> *Moving, running.*

Relay races, the twenty-five yard dash, high jumping.
I was good. The memory elicits tears, hot and burning.
A time of success cut off, forgotten, invisible.
A shadowy recollection of legs running fast, legs
Jumping high, winning.

Did I really go to the citywide competition?
Was it only a wish? Was it only a dream?

I'm alone with an image held tightly in the heart's fist.

Summer was
> roller skating down softly sloping streets
> splashing under water from the backyard garden hose
> freshly washed clothes flapping in the breeze.

Summer was
a family snapshot in black and white:
    the little group of five now
    ever so slightly parted down the middle.

    Dad and Sue—a Pietà;
    His gentle chest a pillow 'round her tiny body,
    His face content and full of smiles.
    Mum's hands resting against the shoulders
    of Marilyn and me
    To form a separate sort of trinity.

Marilyn. The very name evokes an era of easy glamor.
    (Monroe and Maxwell were the way we teased.)
    She, ever so sweetly posed.
    Expressed a dancer's geometry
    In the crossing of one leg over another.
    And the toe ever so graceful against the grass.

    Me, clowning a defense.
    Mum, her spirit face pulling against the camera's sway.

    Not the first or last such picture show.

How well I remember:
    That dress Mum wore:
    German chocolate eyelet, the
    Tidy white pique collar and cuffs
    Like icing 'round her neck and arms.
    Those shoes, high heeled sandals with
    Ankle straps I love to this day;
    Shoes for dancing life's sorrows away.

Soon:
    Recollections mostly of dark, dusk turning to night.
    Halloween.
    Black night lit with jack-o-lantern pumpkins.
    Orange glow and bright kitchen lights cheering
    A waist-high memory:
    Preparations of gypsy clothes—Mum's skirt and blouse,
    Lipstick and colored scarves, bracelets jangle.

Marilyn's face, a perfect Clara Bow.
Suzanne, a rattling baby band.
Feeling the chatter, feeling the laughter, feeling evening.
Balmy, buoyant, free of fear.
Marilyn's hand, a ribbon of play holding mine.
Brown paper shopping bags flying above our shoulders like kites
As our feet danced from house to house,
Our voices ringing bells of trick or treat.
Cinnamon-licked candy apples, Rice Krispies bars,
Pennies and peanut butter "kisses" sorted later
Like gold hoarded and cherished.
Marilyn always keeping hers longer,
Savoring sweetness longer, more knowingly,
The candy against her lips, a mystery play I did not feel.
Halloween, autumn's farewell—after which the street turned cold.

Fear and anger emerge

One white November's eve:
I pack a ball of hard wet snow, and throw it
Into the basement of the corner church
where people are meeting.
I am an eight-year-old loner skulking along Caledonia curbs.
Something in the pinpoint brightness of that light incites me,
And the door opens so easily, then
The ball leaves my hand, its flight down that narrow stairwell
Fast and sure.
Like a skull it smashes, splinters against the floor,
Startles the little group there. They holler and yell ,
                                        "Who?"

I run, panic-stricken,
Home.
Frightened of no one but my father.
Did he know where I am?
No. He's not there.
No one missed me.
The snowball is my secret.

My rage takes form...

Winter 1952
— *Greenlaw Avenue* —

*T*he house

a beauty: solid brick, square floor plan, three stories high. Dad was
selling real estate now, so we began to know the value of property.
It was basic. "Ours is a family of property owners," Dad said.
"Owning property is the most secure form of wealth."

This house resembled Mémère's; smaller, yes, but Mum loved it. In this
house she may have thought she might recapture that which seemed
forever lost.

On the other hand,
Mum remembers:

> Dad had a migraine the day we moved in. He'd get
> a migraine almost every time we moved.

Greenlaw—
a staircase that wound from the first to the second floor—a place
I liked to sit, to hear everything that was going on without
anyone seeing me.

And the best room of all was the sunporch on the second floor, the
room Dad chose for his office at home. With windows all around it,
the sun poured in so warm, and I napped there when I could (like a
cat on crisp winter days). There were so many rooms we rented those
on the top floor out for a while. Dad was enterprising. "The income
will help if sales get slow," he said.

A young couple moved in; they were newly married. It seemed to me
they were always laughing. I sometimes met them on the stairs and
caught them stealing a kiss at every floor. They didn't live with us too
long. They wanted to start a family and needed a bigger place. That's
okay, Mum and Dad thought, it's better without tenants anyway.
Besides, Dad's business was so good we really didn't need the
money.

54

In the basement Dad set up a play area for us. He hung long springs from the ceiling to form a trapeze without a bar.

We hooked our hands into the circular grips at the ends of each coil and imagined ourselves circus performers as we turned somersaults in the air. Dad clearly enjoyed seeing us swing from his latest invention.

Our house here was always open to friends. We were encouraged to bring kids in to play whenever we liked, and did, especially when we became the first ones on the block to have television.
Every Saturday from then on our living room was the local movie theater — Hopalong Cassidy and Howdy Doody came to occupy those mornings.

For a house otherwise large, the kitchen was unusually small—more like a pantry. The ceilings were about thirteen feet high.
Long plate glass doors closed over the tall narrow built-in cup-boards.

Perhaps because we felt so crowded there, the tiny table where we sat for meals became a place where family tensions often smoldered and sometimes even came to a boil. It was there Suzanne and I experienced our first fatal confrontation. She was about two years old then, and one morning she was gleefully splattering her food, waving a spoon defiantly in the air. Dad got annoyed and scolded her. I said to myself he's being too harsh.

Even though Sue was clearly quite ready to defend herself, I, surrogate mother duck that I was, chose to interfere. I told Dad what I wouldn't accept! Sensing I was butting in on her battle,
Sue directed shrill babblings at me and in no uncertain terms staked out her territorial boundaries. "Get out," she seemed to say, "Get out, and go away, you're not needed any more." Sullen, defeated, muttering "Good riddance," I got up from the table and left them alone.

Seeking to ease the break in my heart, I decided to pay a visit to
Elizabeth and Michelle, twins I knew who lived through the alley on the next block over; they were special to me in part because their birthday was the day before mine and somehow that meant to me we were almost sisters.

I liked the way their house sat high up off the street. To reach it,
I had to climb a steep set of stairs. Their front yard was not really a
yard, but a rock garden worked into the sloping ground; hens and
chicks, moss serving in place of grass. We enjoyed playing on those
steps, each one a table for our games or a convenient leaning post for
our elbows as we chatted and teased about boys we liked at school.

That day I couldn't laugh or talk at all. Even the twins couldn't cheer
me up. I was stuck in the darker avenues of my mind, reliving the
guilty remains of an earlier day at Regal Road
School:

> Built of cold grey stone and brick—
> > Fortress-like, the biggest school building yet.
> > I liked it okay, I suppose, but
> > There was a loneliness in me now. And
> > *I must find that pair of gloves.*
>
> > Afraid to tell my mother I'd dropped mine,
> > I went to the Lost & Found
> > And said of one lovely pair,
> > *That's them. They're mine.*
>
> > In fact they weren't, but
> > they were green, the brightest green ever,
> > with a row of diamond shapes in black and yellow,
> > that spread out nicely
> > across the knuckles of my hands.
> > *I'll take these, who's to know?*
>
> > Once out-of-doors, I felt an odd shudder—
> > dusk sucked 'round me.
>
> > *I hate December, the days so*
> > *short. What if I meet the one to whom these*
> > *gloves really belong?*
>
> > No sooner did I have the thought, but she appeared—
> > a girl my age, with gloves exactly like mine.
> > The green gleamed ever more brightly—an emerald
> > In the light of a street lamp I could not avoid.

She's a twin. She knows these
gloves. If she sees, she'll cry
out, 'hey'. . .

Quickly, my hands found my pockets.
With teeth chattering,
head bowed, legs melting ice,
miraculously my feet kept a steady dependable rhythm
forward, and I didn't look back. Before
entering the house I carefully
removed the gloves,
and stuffed them out of sight.
Two days later, I knew in my heart
I must take them back.

The cardboard box they called the Lost & Found
sat in a closet next to the principal's office.
I glanced 'round as I waited for the crowd of kids
to thin, the on-guard teacher to be distracted. Then, I
swiftly slipped in, the gloves secreted up under my
armpits; it took only one more instant to open my coat.
I let them fall back into the box from which they came.
Then, smartly rifling through the pile of
sundry items, I searched for my own lost pair.

DARN! They're still not here.
I haven't time.
Get out.
Go. Now.

Lucky me, no one was around.
It was over. I sauntered on,
free, satisfied.
That evening,
I stole a handful of blackball candies
From the store around the corner where
I went to buy milk for breakfast.

We lived there shy of seven months only because on weekends and evenings the brick buttress that bordered the sidewalk along-side the Greenlaw property became a convenient "bench" for drunk veterans leaving the Legion Hall across the street. Those people Mum called "a bit of unwanted company," and Dad had stronger words to describe.

One night fire sirens woke us and smoke seeped in through our windows. Before we knew it a crowd of frightened people were pounding at the front door, staggering onto the verandah as a big fire raged through that Hall. They were seeking help.

Without hesitation Mum and Dad obliged, permitting them to use the phone, the toilet, providing water. It was a night that got Mum and Dad thinking. Dad, ever restless, ever ready to move on, decided soon after:

>*"It's a good time to sell. Lots of immigrants are*
>*pouring into Toronto. The neighborhood's hot."*

Within no time, it was a done deal.

When school closed June 29, 1952, we were pretty well packed and ready to go.

❖ ❖ ❖ ❖

Summer 1952
— Jane Street —

Dad was flying high, hang-gliding over Toronto real estate.
He enjoyed what they called "speculating": buying property specifically to make a profit. That's why he bought "the duplex."

I heard him explaining:
>It's a good buy; needs some work, but we'll invest.
>The location's good—on the Bloor streetcar line,
>and just out front's the trolley bus. Around the
>corner's all the shopping you need—the butcher,
>the baker, the candlestick maker.

I laughed and replied:
>Oh, Daddy, there's no
>candlestick maker!

By then Dad had a partner. Jo X was from Czechoslovakia; he came to Canada to escape Communism under which his family'd lost everything—their timberlands, their pulp and paper mills. Jo got his start in Toronto selling fine cut lead crystal. He was a big man, even bigger than Dad, who was about 5'10" and 225 pounds at the time. They both loved to laugh and got along real well. In fact, they bought "Jane St." together.

So, Jo and his wife Esther lived in the upstairs apartment, and we lived in the down. Esther spoke sweetly with a low lilting accent.
She was originally from Estonia; she, too, knew the dark side of Communism. A fragrance of roses clung to her. Whenever we met, she took my hand in hers, and bent close to say hello.

It was Esther who introduced us to real European rye bread—the kind that smells of warm vinegar, the kind you slice yourself and smear with thick, sweet butter; the taste alone told me much about the happiness she must have known.

As the Jane Street property had no real front or back yard to play in, and as the house was going to be busy with carpenters and plumbers all summer, Marilyn and I were packed off for a few weeks with Ma in Collingwood.

Then it was on to Chatham—these summer stays would become something of a pattern over the next few years.

These were the sunshine times.

Summer
(as it was)

- 1 -

a.m.

>
> five o'clock, Pépère
> seven o'clock, Mémère
> eight o'clock, us
>
>
> linoleum, morning cool
> scramble to the rag rug
> quick your socks on
> down the back stairs to see
> Pépère coming
> in from the barn
> there he is, see
> through the gate, hear
> there, he's
> down the back steps
> the door clapped
> now, listen
> his feet tap on the linoleum
> then, hear
> nothing, nothing
> > wait   wait
>
> Mémère to the door
> "Bien mon dieu!
> Es-tu en bas là?"
>
> > listen   listen
>
> now, hear
> Pépère comes
> up the stairs for breakfast, and
> there we sit
> smiling on a summer morning.

- 2 -

Monday, wash day

roll out the old wringer
fill it up with water and suds
in go the clothes
whites first
then the darks

"MISÉRABLE!"

and last, the cleaning rags

drain it
fill it again
blue the whites
drain it
"À PERPÈTUITÉ!"

Mémère, a force alone
her muttered curses propelling the day

fill it again
now rinse
first the whites
through the wringer
"get on the other side one of you girls
pull them through,
BE CAREFUL NOW"
rinse the darks
through the wringer
"let them come right through"
and last the cleaning rags rinse
through the wringer
"catch them, on the other side"

now out back to hang

"DIEU MERCI"

MORNING

- 3 -

tin roof'd verandah
Mémère bandannah'd
shaking rag rugs in the air
feathers falling on the trumpet vine—
another morning of chores.
Pépèrelong gone to the fields:

Mémère on the move, in the kitchen 'cause
   "the men'll be coming to eat
      12 o'clock sharp, so

"scrub down the potatoes good,
we'll boil them with their jackets."

   mm.
   Marilyn and I
   the two of us sitting there
   outside on the side steps with
   a big tub of water, and
   the potatoes.

flies buzzing, cows moaning
pigs snorting, wallowing in mud under the sun

   "oh, look, the boats are coming down!"

   from Detroit, pleasure yachts
   casually pass
   up the Thames to Chatham.
   those aboard wave
   to us and the fishermen—
   the fishermen sitting on
   the riverbanks
   beyond the cornfield.

THE ROOT IS BITTER, THE ROOT IS SWEET

Those fishermen were the only black folk we knew then
fishing there beyond the cornfield, sitting on the riverbanks.

> and we were just scrubbing those potatoes
> practically all morning.
> Mémère baking pies
> frying chicken
> (the very one she caught, wrung its neck
> and plunged into boiling water earlier)
>
> and to her garden going
> for corn and salad greens.
>
> 12 o'clock noon
> the table's set, and
> the men do arrive.
>
> tractors parked,
> they head
> for the basement where
> hands and faces are washed.
> then, up the back stairs they trundle
> hungry, ready to eat.

MORNING

- 4 -

threshing time.
men, intense bodies
taut and agile
strumming sustained
concentrated rhythms
among tractors, combines, wagons
of hay the sun hot and crackling.

the hay loft swallows the brittle
glistening stalks
wheat germ fills the granary
children slide beneath the gentle
spray of golden kernels
munching
oblivious.

- *5* -

the house held
on her shadow side
deep in the ground
the humid apple cool fruit cellar
white Queen Anne cherries preserved and crowded
into Mason jars, 'longside
homemade ketchup and tomato juice
jams of rhubarb, peach, and plum
stood waiting for the toast of a
cozy winter morning.

holding, too,
memories of
the Saturday in '51
when she
received
on her pine shaded lawns
family friends
for the wedding of Julienne to Germain Lafontaine
the day I consumed
banana blended peanut butter, tea, sandwiches
and nine bottle of pop!

*S*ometimes while in Collingwood with Ma we'd visit Aunt Eileen.

Eileen was another of Dad's younger sisters: there was Clara, Mabel, Margaret, Eileen and Marion. Dad occupied the number three position among the six children.

Aunt Eileen and Uncle Frank Giffin owned a farm. They specialized in apples and berries, but had several field crops as well. For them the summer was no time to slumber. And, considering they were a family with four young children, there was very little time to spare.

No matter the 'busyness,' they never failed to welcome us warm-ly—their large dark eyes sparkling, their voices singing "hello," their laughter walking us in through the back screen door.

Friday was the day Aunt Eileen took her berries to town. And if we got there early enough in the morning, we'd be allowed to help pick and pack—blueberries, strawberries or raspberries—into pint size boxes. Which berries we chose depended on what was ripe on the vines. Once done, we'd help load the trays into the car—then, scrambling in ourselves, we'd chant:

> *This little piggy goes to market.*
> *This little piggy stays home.*
> *This little piggy buys roast beef.*
> *This little piggy gets none.*

Oh, how I remember
> the ride down the winding lane that led away from the house, the sandy gravel crunching under the wheels and the car swaying like a hammock in the warm mid-morning sun. At the foot of the lane one of us'd get out to open and close the big wire gate. That done, we'd be on our way turning left into the road. About a half a mile down we'd take a right, passing through a little village in the valley of Devil's Glen where we'd wave and toot the horn at anyone standing in the General Store door. One more hill and that was that. The rhythm of the curves, the slow amble of the drive filled me with a sense of belonging. With the sun looking directly at me through the dense woods as we passed I felt safe and happy.

In Collingwood our main stop was Monroe's Grocery, the same
store Ma called to order her grocery supplies every week. It was
also the store Uncle John referred to when, lowering his voice to
a whisper, he'd tease us saying:

> I'll get you girls a job this summer.
> Do you wanta know what it is?
>
> Pickin' fly dirt outta the bins,
> down at Monroe's.

We'd wince, giggle and weakly protest:

> Oh, Uncle John!
> That's horrible!

That joke was bad, but not as bad as
another one he liked to repeat:

> You girls need a summer job?
> How 'bout I get you one at the
> Chinese laundry? . . .
> Beatin' farts outta bed sheets.

With his teasing words in the back of our minds, it was a holler
to be at Monroe's with Aunt Eileen on 'official business,' and we
had a real hoot pretending we were farm girls in town for the day.

❖ ❖ ❖ ❖

*S*aturday night there was often a wiener roast at Uncle Frank's.

After dark, once the men were back from the fields and had time to wash up, Uncle Frank might build a bonfire half way down the lane, well away from the house. A big crowd would gather: neighboring farmers, their kids, a dog or two.

Night at Uncle Frank's was really night—black and warm with the fire, the stars, house and barn lights flickering a secret shared delight.

One such Saturday night Mum and Dad were up for the weekend. Dad had his guitar and harmonica. Everyone gathered 'round, singing, young and old alike:

> *The farmer in the dell*
> *The farmer in the dell*
> *Hi-ho, the derry-o*
> *The farmer in the dell*

We all joined in forming a circle to play:

> *The farmer takes a wife*
> *The farmer takes a wife*
> *Hi-ho, the derry-o*
> *The farmer takes a wife*
>
> *The wife takes a child*
> *The wife takes a child*
> *Hi-ho, the derry-o*
> *The wife takes a child*

Wieners roasting, marshmallows toasting—
It was one time I'd never forget . . .

Someone knew Mum had a fine voice, and asked:
    Give us a song, Jeanne. *Ave Maria.*

    Mum:
        Oh, no. Not now.

THE ROOT IS BITTER, THE ROOT IS SWEET

Yes. Yes. I insist.

> No, please. Thanks,
> but not now.

Come on, Jeanne, you must!

Dad strummed the opening chords on the guitar:
> Yes, Jeanne, you must!

> *Ave Maria!*
> *Gratia plena*
> *Maria, gratia plena*

There was a drunk in the crowd. He staggered near:
> What the fuck's goin' on here.
> Who wants to hear her sing that!
> Shut the fuck up!

People were upset:
> No, Jeanne, don't listen to him.
> Get that drunk out of here.
> Go on Jeanne, sing.

> *Maria, gratia plena*
> *Maria, gratia plena*
> *Ave, Ave! Dominus*

> Who's drunk? Not me. Get your hands offa me.
> I say, shut that bitch the fuck up!

Dad got mad, stood up:
> Why, you bastard; you don't talk to
> my wife like that and get away with it.

The drunk moved toward Dad, ready to fight.

There was a tussle as the men tried pulling
the drunk back; all the while
he ranted on:

MORNING

God damn that woman. Who wants to hear
that shit! "Ave Maria." GO TO HELL! Is she
French? Someone told me the bitch is French.

Uncle Frank managed to pull him off to the side:
        If anyone's getting out of here, it's you, old man.

Other people consoled Mum:
        I'm so sorry, Jeanne.
        Me, too. Who's that nut anyway?
        You have such a lovely voice.
        It's a crying shame I tell you.
        I so love to hear you sing.

She responded quietly:
        Thank you.
        But I knew it wasn't
        the place for me to be singing,
        not that song.

Dad said, sharply:
        To hell with him.

People started to leave.
Heads turned, eyes grew dark.
There was a throbbing in my throat
My stomach felt full of ants
My ears burned.
I wanted to scream, but didn't.

Dad tried to recover the good spirit of the evening:
        Come on now, where are . . .
        come on kids, let's play . . .
        Join hands again for the mouse.
        You forgot the mouse. Remember:

        The mouse takes the cheese
        The mouse takes the cheese

The fire no longer felt warm.
The flames were feeble and low.
I wished Dad would've stopped playing, but no:

Hi-ho, the derry-o
The mouse takes the cheese

Come on now, you can't all leave me here.

Someone else said:
            Oh, it's getting late, anyway.

Still Dad sang:

The cheese stands alone
The cheese stands alone
Hi-ho, the derry-o
The cheese stands alone

One fool monkey's not ruining
this show! Come on now, everybody.
Let's have one more song:

Someone laughed, patted Dad
on the back. He changed the tune
and sang, sweetly

I dream of Jeannie
. . .

No one joined in.
            Oh come on now, don't everyone
            go home.

The bitterness, the sweetness forever entwined.

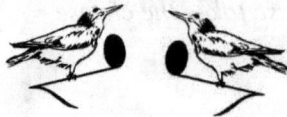

We got back to Toronto late August (1952)
in time to get ready for school.
How many's that, now?
Five schools—Fourth Grade.
Every year a new one?
They were becoming a blur.
We recited their names like they were chimes on a clock:
Fern Avenue, Danforth, Hughes, Regle Road,
now Runnymede.

Dad was on a roll. He was moving fast;
life was to be lived at a fever pitch—
told us he had a brand new Cadillac on order. Plus, he'd
bought a small Austin and hired a chauffeur, Bob!

Among the oral history questions I ask is:

> Mum, what was
> going on then?
> Oh, gosh. Dad would go through different phases.

"Different phases"—
her euphemism for the
manic-depressive cycles
she knows so much more
about than we did as
children—after all, this
was still the morning of
our lives—only with the
darkness at noon would
we begin to see what
the night held in store.

He was getting tired of driving himself around.

I imagine his words:
> It's easier to sell
> when you don't have to
> be fighting with traffic.
> Shifting gears in

that Austin's not easy.
I'm working sun up to
sun down, and the nights
are so noisy. Who'd have
thought we'd be living on
a goddamn truck route!
Oh, well, I only bought
to sell, anyway. You'll
see, we'll be moving from
here, soon.

Mum tells me:

People thought it was so funny. "Brandon's got a
chauffeur. Really!" they'd say.

I remember:

The day the Cadillac arrived Dad
took us for a test drive—up
Jane, along Annette, down Bloor
and back. Everyone was looking.
Dad's smile was as warm and as wide
as the September sun.
The car was a robin's egg blue
(like the eggs he collected when he
was a boy). Long and sleek with
modest fins, it floated 'round
corners like a fish, drove
like a dream.

Mum hated the car.
It was too long, too showy for her.
Dad's grandiosity was getting Mum's goat.
She vowed he'd see her dead
before he caught her driving that car!
She wanted other things more,
Like a permanent home.

She adds to the history:

I could drive, but I just didn't like that car. And
I didn't particularly like the Austin either.

74

(She'd have found fault with any car—and with good reason, too. Dad had a maniacal love of speed. Although he never had an accident, being in a car with him when the spirit moved him to dart in and out of city traffic, or to scoot up the shoulder of a highway at top speed to bypass a bottleneck was to be a hostage in a domestic reign of terror.)

> So, even though he'd hired Bob for himself, Dad decided I should use him instead. I wasn't that keen on it, but Dad insisted so there I was! Around that time, I got the idea I'd like to earn some money of my own.

For all his success, Dad was never generous with his money. That we had a roof over our heads and food on the table he thought should be enough. Pocket money was something we (Mum included) didn't need to have.

Mum continues:

> I inquired around, and heard about different things in sales. One option was these pots and pans— Westbend Stainless Steel. I'd go out for a few hours in the mornings after you and Marilyn had gone to school. Bob (the chauffeur) would drive, and Suzanne'd stay with him in the car while I went knocking on doors. We'd get back to serve your lunch. Dad would often come home then, too. I didn't stick at it long. I thought it looked a little ridiculous—me with a chauffeur, selling pots and pans. It didn't feel too promising.

— *February* —

Bob sent Mum a
Valentine/Birthday card.
It was beautifully scrolled, and
addressed her as "My Darling."
Dad was very angry: "What did
he intend, sending you a card
like that?"

Bob was fired! Being nothing to her,
Mum certainly didn't care.

Around April, Dad sold the Jane St.
property. Jo X was away at the time,
but Mum remembers it well:
        The deal was very sweet. When Dad told Jo the
        big profit they'd made, Jo gave him a great big
        hug.

Naturally, we had to move.
Dad already had a place he'd
bought, again on speculation.
It was a commercial property
this time, right downtown,
on Beaconsfield—off Dundas,
east of Dufferin.

Spring 1953
— Beaconsfield Avenue —

*I*t was mid-May when we actually left Jane Street. With little more than a month still to go at school, Marilyn and I rose each day before dawn so we'd be ready to go by streetcar back to Runnymede. Leaving before it was light felt a little scary; plus it happened to be a very rainy spring, so the mornings were especially dark and gloomy. But Mum bought us new raincoats, and for some reason that, and the responsibility of traveling on our own, gave me a dubious sense of importance. Somewhere inside I knew this ride signaled a new phase in life, a new relationship with my parents, a greater responsibility for the protection of myself and my sister. I received this knowledge soberly, my feet solidly fixed on the ground.

The streetcar took us past the Junction along Dundas, through a light industrial zone; with its warehouses and other grimly appointed brick buildings, it could have been a forgettable stretch except for the sweet, sweet smell of simmering chocolate gently waking our half-asleep noses as it wafted up from one of those factories.

Coming back in the afternoons was easier than going off in the mornings. I felt genuine relief reaching home knowing that nothing bad had happened to me or Marilyn in between.

Home was now this odd piece-of-pie shaped building, its broad front narrowing to nothing in back. On ground level was a vacant grocery storefront that Dad immediately set about fixing for his new partnership—The Brandon Turner Real Estate and Insurance Company. The floor was ancient and splintered. Ripping it up did wonders. Actually this renovation was the first stage in preparing for resale, which was the real reason for buying.

Mum says:

> People thought Dad was really crazy this time.
> They were sure he'd get stung on this one, even
> with his reputation. They used to say, "If there's
> an old place hard to sell, give it to Brandon."
>
> And getting rid of this place, oh boy, it wasn't
> easy!

With its lovely broad bay windows, it didn't take all that much to make the store really nice. The two living floors above, however, were less easy to transform.

Mum hated the place:

> I had to wash that kitchen floor every day, and the rag I
> used to do it with would be black, black!
> People were still heating with coal, see, and there was a
> coal furnace in that basement. The soot was terrible. I
> wouldn't even think of hanging my clothes outside to
> dry. Then, too, the rooms were small and oddly shaped,
> like the building they narrowed from front to back.
> Everything felt so congested. We were afraid of being
> trapped up there in the bedrooms on the third floor.

Dad rigged up ropes near our bed. Big heavy duty ropes. He showed us how we could lower ourselves out the window and climb down should there be a fire.

Not only was that the hottest summer I can ever remember, but also there was a polio scare and everyone was put on alert. Mum worried about us picking up germs: "Don't look down sewers, don't even breathe the air around them," she warned.

For Marilyn and me, every new place held its charms, and we sort of flowed into new games and activities as the space inspired us. Because our bedroom here accommodated only one bed without much room to spare, our two beds became one. With the mat-tresses piled one on top of the other, a play area was created, perfect for rolling and trampoline-style jumping.

At this age she and I were probably as close as we'd ever be. Our feelings for each other were very deep, and we explored our emerging curiosity about sex together on that bed quite naively. Take the afternoon we'd been to see "Pickup On South Street," a real *film noir*, very lurid, about gangsters and Communist agents, starring Richard Widmark. He'd slug his girlfriend, knock her to the floor; then, with blood still oozing down her cheeks, they'd fall into a passionate embrace. No sooner home and there we were reenacting that scene. With a handkerchief between our lips, we kissed and hugged, laughing uproariously, billing and cooing, playacting the fight, and kissing some more.

Drama was our preoccupation that summer (and to become an actress was my secret ambition). With Mum so scared of what the streets might have held, we mainly played indoors, our living room a theater, the stage area marked off with sheets over chairs.
Charging neighborhood kids to come in, we earmarked the money for donation to the Red Cross. Our plan was to hold these "club" events once a week throughout the summer and send the money collected in at the end. But that plan got interrupted when Mum and Dad decided to get out of the city and take a trip across "the States" to California with Aunt Margaret and Uncle Hubert.

Mum's oral history account
fills me in on facts about Margaret
I've either forgotten, or in fact
never did know:

>   Aunt Margaret had just been released from The Ontario
>   Hospital, where she'd been treated for severe
>   depression. Dad suggested the trip thinking a change of
>   scenery might cheer her up.

>   Margaret didn't speak a word for the first several days
>   we traveled.

Marilyn, Suzanne and I stayed those few
weeks with Pépère and Mémère.

- 1 -

Do you remember, Pépère?
    do you remember
    the day in late July
    Mum and Dad set out in the blue
    Cadillac, bound for California
    and you dared that noon
    to criticize him, my father?

        "Just when do you think you'll settle down,
        stop this everlasting movement? Can't you stay
        put anywhere more than six months?"

dared to mock his spirit?

        "Why the hell would you want to
        follow that Mormon John Smith's
        route West? What do you think you're
        going to find in Salt Lake City? No
        God I want anything to do with.
        You've got some strange notions,
        a dreamer's cockeyed schemes is all
        they are, if you ask me."

dared, before us, his children?
and, just as it seemed the two of you
might fight, fight like you did
one snow-white midnight past
full fisted fighting
so awful, the moon went out,
I reared at you.
reared my body, and my voice
against you
against your mockery
in defense of my Daddy,
that man through whom I know the
two faces of God—creator and destroyer—
and your eyes exploded
in mine, on fire.
and you did back off.

80

- 2 -

Sunday
       waking reluctantly

the incense'd air of L'IMMACULÉE CONCEPTION
luring us from sleep
               Mass at 10:00 a.m.

awkwardly dressing
plunking white straw hats—
purchased for Easter, the rims
now misshapen
the flowers crushed, and askew—
atop our Protestant heads.

once at church,
secretly enjoying the mystery of the mass
wishing to be part of the ritual kneelings and prayers
rapidly sung 'long rosaries of gold and pearl.
crying somewhere inside for the Lost Paradise,
and soothed by the passion of Bach.

longing for our own first communion veil
never to be.

the communion out of bounds
               to us, child heretics.

and wondering why
the priest spoke so harshly against
                   mixed marriage.

*S*eptember
I turned ten on the 3rd
and school began, again.

No one,
neither Mum nor Marilyn quite remembers—
was the school Sir Adam Beck, or Alexander Muir?

Who cares?
We went there only three weeks.
Yes, that's right.

I can hear Mum saying:
> We'll be moving soon. This place is not yet sold, but
> while you girls were away, the deal went through on a
> brand new house. It's a bungalow in the suburbs, all the
> way West, past Jane— Islington. You'll like it, I know
> you will. It's got a big backyard, three bedrooms, a
> basement; Dad wants to fix up a rec room. I want to buy
> you girls new pleated plaid skirts and navy blazers. I
> always think young girls look so nice in the classic
> styles.

The only person I remember from Beaconsfield is a boy; a boy
whose name I don't recall, just that he was in my class. Newly
immigrated from some Eastern European country, he wore old-
fashioned, heavy wool tweed knickers (despite the heat of
September). The kids teased him mercilessly about his clothes.
Poor soul. One day, too afraid, I suppose, to hold up his hand
and be excused, he wet on himself. Someone seeing the pool of
piss streaming along the floor told the teacher. She tried to be
discreet, but when he got up to leave the room, his wool pants
drenched and stained, everyone could see what'd happened.
Many giggled. I choked back tears.

I, too, knew the trauma of displacement.

> *Go in and out the window,*
> *Go in and out the window,*
> *Go in and out the window,*
> *As we have done before.*

That was it for the Red Cross 'club.'
The money let's see . . .
one, two dollars . . .
and ten, fifteen, forty cents.
Oh, heck, what's the Red Cross
going to do with this little
bit of money?

> *Go up and down the staircase,*
> *Go up and down the staircase,*
> *Go up and down the staircase,*
> *As we have done before.*

Might as well keep it. Don't tell.
No, that's not right. Better
have one more meeting. Give it back.

> *Go stand and face your partner,*
> *Go stand and face your partner,*
> *Go stand and face your partner,*
> *As we have done before.*

Say goodbye.

Dolores (left) Suzanne, Marilyn.
Collingwood, Ontario 1953

Noon

Fall 1953

Little did we know
to how much we were saying goodbye
as we settled in
on Goswell Road—the place we call home to this day.
Little did we know that Dad's working days were numbered,
that the migraine headaches that occurred with each move
were warnings
of much deeper troubles to come,
that depression would roll in on him
like fog and settle for years.

❖ ❖ ❖ ❖

Yes, the house was just as was promised—
    a pretty red brick bungalow,
    green roof, white trim,
    three bedrooms,
    an attached garage.
    Built by the Longo Brothers.
    Cost—$17,000.
    Dad paid cash.

Inside
    hardwood floors—beautiful, freshly waxed—
    a wonderful surface to slide along as
    Mum chattered on about drapes and furniture,
    and Dad "sold" us on the importance of the corner lot:
        "It's always the most valuable."
    And, of the basement,
        "Never buy a house without one."

He, you understand, had speculation on his mind,
whereas Mum was determined to stay put!
And we did, though life here would be far from
entirely stable.

87

Out
    lovely large picture windows, we surveyed the surrounding land.
    Formerly an orchard,
    This subdivision had been bulldozed clear
    except for the odd fruit tree here and there.
    We were lucky. We had three in our yard—
    two pears, one old and hollow,
    plus one young plum.
    We valued those trees like gold.
    Many a neighboring house had nothing growing or green,
    nothing to break the overall bleakness.

❖ ❖ ❖ ❖

First thing on the agenda for Marilyn and me, of course, was school.

— *Wedgewood Public* —

It was a sprawling one-storey yellow brick structure with wings.
Very different from the sturdy old monuments we'd attended
before.

Miss Ballard was my teacher:
    "Too bad you weren't able to start out with us
    at the beginning of the year.
    We're a month under way,
    hope you won't have too much trouble fitting in."

Not a very warm welcome, I thought.
    Fortunately, the first lesson was double digit division,
    I'd learned that already downtown.
    Whizzing through without a mistake
    I thought I'd saved face, but
    Miss Ballard didn't seem phased. I guessed I was
    just another body in the classroom, and
    she didn't like me.

For that matter, I didn't like myself much anymore.
I wore glasses.
Boys there called me four eyes.
I felt ugly.

Glasses—they were a bane in my life in more ways than that one.
They hid the feature on my face Daddy used to sing about.
You know the song, the one that goes—
Beautiful beautiful brown eyes,
I'll never love blue eyes again.

Of course I knew it was just a song
sung to bring a smile to my face
when I had been crying.
After all he loved Marilyn and Mum, too,
and they both had blue eyes.
Suzanne had brown eyes like me
and—he'd always love her.

What I didn't understand is why
what once inspired song
now only brought shame.

Each time I needed new glasses my eyes had grown weaker.
Then, as if I was more specimen than girl, optometrists talked
over, around and about me. With surprise and shock they'd
declare
    "Oh my, her glasses are going to have to be a lot thicker."

And,
"She has a much wider face than most children her age.
We'll have to find a frame in the adult selection."

I wanted to ask,
    Am I just a full moon face floating here between you?

But, what was the use!

That year Dad'd already decided not to buy new frames at all.
"I'll just dye the clear plastic pair you have.
There's nothing wrong with them,
they're just a little discolored."

He was so full of himself and his inventiveness
as he poured the RIT powder into a pot of boiling water
and dipped my old frames in.
I watched as they turned indigo, praying they'd melt
but no, they just softened enough to bend slightly
and when dried they sat crooked on my face.
He made an effort to correct this but didn't succeed.
In the end I just had to wear them
regardless of the flaws.

> *I'm a butterfly struck with a dart.*

Mummy, where were you then?
What were you thinking?
You used to take such care.
Where oh where was your "pretty little girl"?
Was it because Dad was forever saying,
"I'm the boss here, and don't you forget it"?
Were you very afraid of him then?

No answer.
And, the oral history interviews
bog down with questions like these.

Later that year, his authoritarian arm ever lengthening,
he decided hairdressers were a waste of money,
and took over the cutting of our hair.
He couldn't wait to get at
my lovely long silky brown braids.

> Oh, Mummy, what of the lavender ribbons?

Give me one good reason why my braids have to go.
So what if most girls are wearing theirs short?
So what, so what, so what!

NOON

My tears and cries were for nothing;
like autumn crocus
my braids did fall.

Mum, you remember those cuts?
They were always uneven,
making it hard to figure out exactly
where to draw the part,
where to place the barrette
to ensure the hair would lay evenly on both sides.
Without fail there was always
one piece that just wouldn't fall where I wanted it.

Oh Marilyn, how I envied you—
his rough scissor strokes didn't ruin your curls—
and Suzanne, at two
you looked quite sweet with your Dutch girl bob.
Lucky, lucky both of you,
no glasses to clutter up your pretty faces.

Winter 1954

Ma Brandon's landlord and neighbor died.

Ma'd been renting her house on Beech Street
for the last twenty years.
With this death she might have moved
back into the small white stucco cottage
she owned next door,
the one she'd inherited when her father died,
the tiny house in which she'd given birth
to all six of her children,
the one that was providing her
a small rental income.

    With the estate eager to sell off this asset,
    Dad considered it a very good time to buy.
    He was concerned for Ma's comfort
    (he loved his mother dearly,
    that was for sure).
    Her eyesight was very poor and
    moving would require a very big adjustment.

Unable to consider buying the property for herself,
Dad approached his sisters suggesting they go in together.
They said no.
Dad set about buying it on his own.

    Why his sisters said no,
    and why they didn't approve of his doing so,
    I have no idea.
    We children were never too privy to the details of
    that family's quarrels.
    All of the Brandons could be very tight-lipped.

I do know it had something to do with the chicanery of
Ma's step-siblings—
step-siblings who'd cheated her
out of her rightful inheritance many years before.

Even now, one stepsister was doing all she
could to compromise Ma's fate again,
doing her best to get her hands on this real
estate deal. She wouldn't succeed though.
Dad was as smart as she and a lot more honest.

But the whole mess threw Dad into a depression,
deeper than any we'd known. He complained bitterly:
"This suburban real estate market is so slow and dull!
I hate living in the sticks! I want to move back to the city."

Predictably, Mum said,
      "No, I won't go! And that's that!"

A battle line was drawn.
Dad was held tightly in the destructive arms of
God, and there was no letting go.
He became a real bully.
We could do nothing but obey
his storm force demands.

Like when it was really cold and
the windows weeped with excessive condensation.
He decided the solution was
to turn down the heat,
shut off all the vents in the house during the day,
close all doors, live in the kitchen.

> *Imagine a table round*
> *Mother, father, daughters three*
> *No talking here aloud*
> *Silent undercurrents of rage*
> *Throats locked in sinews of scorn*

And his way was the only way it was ever going to be!

Suffering insomnia, he
tried reading his way to sleep,
choosing history books which told of the Irish famines
that brought his forebears to Canada.
Believing we were to face a shortage of food,

he decided to store fifty pound bags of potatoes
and equally large sacks of onions in the basement.
As winter progressed, the tubers sprouted.
Pinching them clean every few weeks was a task assigned to
Marilyn and me.

> *One potato, two potato, three potato, four*
> *Ahhhhhh*
> *Shboom, shboom. Life could be a dream!*

Interpreting our play as criticism, he
lectured us on the need for austerity;
"You laugh now, but I'll have the last laugh
when these potatoes are all we have to eat!"

> *A miasma at night,*
> *the vapors of his anger*
> *creep through cracks under doors,*
> *weaving open my sleep.*
> *There's a tussle, a thump*
> *and I know it's*
> *Mum's body falling to the floor.*
>
> *Oh God why this? When will it end?*
> *Please have them send me away—*
> *boarding school, that's what I want.*
> *Please God,*
> *tell Daddy to send me away,*
> *anything, anything but this.*
> *Please God, talk to Daddy,*
> *tell him to forgive Mummy,*
> *forget whatever she did wrong.*
> *Please God, please.*

Like most prayers, this one went unanswered.
Mum increasingly looked sad.
He chastised her for it, saying,
"What's wrong with you
you always look mad!"

94

Then there were days he was utterly silent.
A punishing, impenetrable silence.

> *Oh God,*
> *this kitchen's a coffin.*
> *Please, open the doors.*

And the miracle was Marilyn, Suzanne and I,
resilient as winter wrens, did fly—
playing outside for hours,
skating on frozen puddle ponds in the hydro field up the street,
hauling our toboggans to the golf course nearby.

On really good snow days
we laid our bodies on the down-white ground,
spread our arms like wings,
leaving imprints the shape of angels in the soft deep drifts.

*T*oday, wanting to understand as much as I can,
hoping to piece together the factors in his past
that helped make Dad who he was, I wonder
about his childhood. It's obvious he loved Ma,
would do anything for her, but what of his Dad?

Mum says he almost never spoke of him,
rarely mentioned his name.

I decided to interview my cousin, Joan Lee,
(daughter of Margaret, Dad's younger sister,
the one we now know suffered
manic-depressive illness like he).

Joan Lee remembers what
everyone else was keen to forget:

> Grandpa Brandon had a terrible temper.
> Ma wouldn't talk about him. No one wanted to talk about him.
> Margaret would shudder at the mention of his name.
>
> He was extremely violent.
>
> There's one story in particular I was told happened when the
> children were very small.
>
> It seems one evening Ma wasn't getting supper on the table fast
> enough for his liking; no sooner had she set the platter of pork
> chops on the table he, in a rage, picked it up, threw the whole
> dinner on the floor. She was devastated.

Aunt Marion, Dad's youngest
sister, offers more clues....

Ma and Grandpa Brandon on their wedding day, 1907.
Christopher John Brandon and Annie Laura Hughes.

We all had to perform duties around the house. Alvin, being the only son, had to split wood for the stove, and be sure to have kindling for lighting the fire. He had to hoe the garden, mow the lawn, shovel the snow. But as a teenager he got quite involved with a variety of clubs—the Cadets, the collegiate football team. He taught himself music and played trumpet in Collingwood's Kiltie Marching Band. He even had a job as projectionist at the first movie theater in town.

> With all this activity, he wouldn't always get his home chores done, and this infuriated our father. Then, too, Alvin liked to hang around the pool room at times with some of his friends. Pa thought that was an expensive waste of time.

> I recall instances when Ma could see that Alvin wasn't going to get the wood split in time and she'd do it for him to save a scene. Ma was a very gentle person and hated trouble.

Ma's life with Christopher was a
sad life right from the start,
according to Joan Lee.

> Grandpa (Christopher) Brandon was a well-to-do man in his early thirties when he came to Collingwood. He met Ma, then Annie Laura Hughes, at the Trinity United Church.

> They married in 1907. She was twenty-five. He was thirty-four. Ma always said the first thing she imagined when he proposed were pots of geraniums for the window sills of the home he promised to build.

That didn't happen right off,
though.

> Christopher decided he wanted to seek his fortune as a pioneer in the West. So, in 1909 with their newborn infant, Clara, they set out with a few others from Collingwood to claim their plot of Crown Land in Maple Creek, Saskatchewan.

It was no idle pipe dream.

No strangers to suffering, the Brandons had left Ireland destitute after the famines, but with hard work became successful pioneers in Ontario. They were among the first families to open the land around Fenlon Falls, and one John Brandon, a miller, is credited with establishing that town.

But, nothing had prepared Ma for the hardships she was about to meet in Maple Creek. She'd never experienced the total absence of creature comforts and had never known the haunting isolation she was to live through on the prairies.
Homesteads were far apart. There were times when Ma'd be left alone overnight, as Grandpa had more than a day's journey by horse and wagon to obtain building materials and household goods.

She despised everything about that life.

They stayed only six months, leaving Maple Creek when a physical and behavioral regression in young Clara's development, which until then had been entirely normal, became disturbingly obvious. Clara was no longer able to pull herself up to standing with the aid of a chair. Instead she was falling, her little body crumpling to the floor.

Clara even stopped speaking words she'd clearly mastered. Hoping to get medical help, Ma and Grandpa returned to Collingwood. Unfortunately, despite visits to many, many doctors, a cure was never found. No one knows for sure, but it seems it was either cerebral palsy or Rhett syndrome. From then on—incontinent, pre-verbal—Clara was cared for at home the rest of her twenty-five years.

I believe
Dad carried Clara's image
with him always,
like an egg, an emblem of
life's fragility.

> Clara died in 1934. Dad was twenty-one.
> A month so later, Christopher died.

Alvin Brandon (trumpet), 1937.

Alvin Brandon, member of the Kingston Flying Club,
February, 1938.

Dad came of age in the depths of the Depression. When the stock market crashed in 1929, he was sixteen.

Aunt Marion remembers:
Forced to quit school, Alvin's recognized abilities as a graphic artist quickly got him a job at the shipyards as an apprentice draftsman under the mentorship of a man he very much liked.

However, the Depression hit shipbuilding hard and the Yards soon closed putting both him and Pa out of work. There were few jobs. Men counted themselves lucky if they could get a day's work picking apples in nearby orchards.

Mum adds:
Whatever money he earned, Alvin gave to his mother.
The family sometimes supported itself on the paper route he'd established in high school: at one time or another every one of the girls, even Ma, kept it going.

He was trying,
always trying so hard

The one opportunity available?
The Army.
They promised him a place in the band.

November 9, 1936 he joined,
would serve two tours.
The first, in the motor transport division,
ended April 16, 1938.

Joan Lee adds background:

That June (1938) Grandpa Hughes, Ma's father, died. They say his estate was one of the largest ever probated in the county.

Except for the little white stucco cottage,
Ma saw none of that wealth. The step-children took it all.

A thief he will rob you
And take what you have.

What with the death of Christopher and Clara two
years earlier, and now Grandpa Hughes, tragedy was
coming boom, boom, boom!

Canada (and the world) was on the verge of war.
Dad's second enlistment started September 7, 1939.
He would never see battle:

> upon hearing his company was to be sent overseas,
> terror struck. Fear of dying brought on a nervous
> breakdown. He went AWOL, was declared medically
> unfit and by December 20 that same year was given an
> honorable medical discharge. The die was cast.

> *Shame never forgets*
> *Shame talks incessantly*

From this point forward , his mind, ever fragile as
new ice, fractured again and again.

*W*inter '54 was a window on the future.
Seeking solace within, Dad began writing verse:

> *Tears unlike the rain*
> *With salt are kissed and scent*
> *The dew is pure*

> *While tears are filled*
> *With love, with grief*
> *Advent.*
> *Be still wild heart*
> *Beat not full on*
> *Be quiet in the night*
> *Remember God*

> *Whose Son has said*
> *Fear not, Thy Faith*
> *Is might.*

To that gentle aspect of Dad's soul I cleaved
through hell and high water in the years to come.

102

Spring 1954

Dad closed the deal on Ma's house March 27, 1954
with $3,500 cash.
I remember how proud I was:
    "It's so wonderful," I thought,
    "that he could and would do that for his mother.
    It's a true measure of his character!"

"Now my girls will always have a home," he said.

Though none of us ever did go there to live,
I know we all cherish memories of time spent in
that pretty pale sienna brick center hall two-floor
with its widow's peak, the backyard a short quarter acre,
fenced in with a row of singing poplars.

That house and fond thoughts of Ma were constants
in a life otherwise quite unpredictable.

    Oh, my dear Ma,
    You who wished never
    to be called Grandma,
    But preferred to protect
    An illusion of self
    Always young,
    Never going past the age
    Of motherhood—
    How I remember you:
    Locked behind those pale
    Blue, scarred eyes—
    Spectacl'd, straining, ever
    Shaded from the sun,
    Watching us from under
    A cupped hand
    Or visor'd headpiece.

    That dainty laugh
    Floating across your taut
    Lips at the sight of a

Melting ice cream cone.
And the fragrant red hawthorn tree
Where you'd sit with us
In July.

Those July days:
The grass beginning to scorch
Under foot,
The plantain ever more haughty,
And the peony heads heavy.
You, poised and shy as lily-of-the-valley;
Your voice always subdued.

We'd serve the noon time meal
At the shipyard's whistle,
Keep it hot on the wood-fired stove
Ready for table
When Aunt Mabel and Uncle John'd come
Bicycling in by Mr. Parrot's drive,
And with a "how d'ya do"
Waltz through
The woodshed door—hungry
For lunch, fresh from
The garden out back:
Potatoes, tender as tickles,
Carrots, melting with butter, and black pepper.
Ham sweet, and
Warm milk pudding with raspberries.

The morning granted us
Lazy afternoons.
We'd dry our rain wash'd hair
In the sun.
Still holding the memory of hand
Laced pillow slips
And sheets cumulus cool
Against warm sun-baked shins.
(Never would you be known
to place less than perfect
linen on the beds of your home.)

NOON

At dusk
We'd entertain
In the woodshed.
Marilyn might sing,
Imitating Al Jolson
With great charm
And applause.

Sometimes, late at night there'd be
A thunder storm:
Fearful of lightening,
You'd wake us and
Take us with you down
To the kitchen to sit
By the screen door, open.
You, rocking in the dark;
We, crosslegg'd at your feet, or one
Combing through your long white hair—
You loved us to comb through;
Your eyes softly closed.
How I remember you:
Other evenings, sitting
Proper as a pocket handkerchief
In the back of that black Dodge
Four door,
Hands folded, and still
Shading your eyes squinted
Against the setting sun
As we went riding,
Riding away.

Oh, my dear Ma.

— As 1954 ends —

Dad, inspired by a book on the life of the Trapp family, decided we should develop our familial music talents, and set about organizing us. Our material included songs from the Frank Loesser musical, *Hans Christian Anderson.*

At Dad's insistence we gathered every day to practice in the dining room. That's where the piano now stood—the solid mahogany upright Grand given to us by Pépère and Mémère when we'd moved to Greenlaw. The piano Mum had learned to play on when she was a girl.

I remember
Dad arranging us in two rows—
Mum and I behind, Suzanne and Marilyn up front.

Then, him lecturing:
> *The key to success is discipline. Failure is simply a matter of not enough discipline. It's discipline that won the Second World War and lack of discipline meant the Titanic sank. Discipline's what got Brigham Young and the Mormons to Salt Lake City. Remember that when we practice.*

We'd hear this kind of talk a lot as Dad played the chords on the piano and assumed a drill sergeant persona in his role as Music Director.

I still have the book with his hand-written chord sequences etched in above the notes. I still pause when I see those pen strokes made with a dreamer's certainty and an optimistic poise. I still carry within me the wonder I felt in the presence of his mind—a mind once so free, so unfettered. I see the freedom in the chord letter names—F, C#, Dim6, Dm. He didn't just play the notes, he felt them, lived in the rhythms, danced in the abstract.

Remember
> Dad taught himself to read music,
> played trumpet in Collingwood's
> Kiltie Marching Band, joined the
> Army on a promise he'd play in their band,
> and did. He'd also joined Herb Dixon's

Dance Band, and at one point even organized
his own, playing at Wasaga Beach night clubs.

No question, he had an ear for music.

But . . .
I was eleven years old, and given the hostility my inferior abilities as
a singer elicited, I wasn't particularly interested in this family
venture. Plus, the military approach provoked a rebelliousness in me I
found hard to conceal, singing the verses of Inch Worm:

> *Two and two are four, four and four are eight*
> *That's all you have on your business-like mind.*

Marilyn had the melody line,
I was supposed to hold the harmony with
Mum, but my concentration drifted,
I lost my place and fell into unison with Marilyn.

Dad got impatient:
> No. No. Forget the melody,
> Dolores, keep to your own note.
> Like this.

He played more forcefully, singing my part:

> *Two and two are four, four and four are eight,*
> *How can you be so blind?*

Demanding:
> Hear it. Get it.
> Okay, do it again,

> *Two and two are four, four and four are eight*
> *That's all you have on your business-like mind.*
> *Two and two are four, four and four are eight*
> *How can you be so blind?*

'Cuz I have four eyes! (I told myself.)
Good. Now, let's keep going,

Inch worm, inch worm, measuring the marigolds
You and your arithmetic, you'll probably go far.

> Dolores, stay with me now.
> Listen to the harmony.

Inch worm, inch worm measuring the marigolds,
Seems to me, you'd stop and see how beautiful they are.

My voice had no lilt,
my spirit was heavy.

> No. No. No.
> Let's just do your part, Dolores.
> Help her Jeanne.
> I'll play only the alto line.
> Listen, first.

He played, and sang:

> *Inch worm, inch worm . . .*

I interrupted, insisting:
> It's too low for me. The teacher who directs the choir at school
> put me in with the sopranos. She says I'm definitely a soprano,
> and she tested every one of us singing by ourselves.

> What you do with her has nothing to do with what I'm doing
> here. I want Marilyn to do that part. Jeanne, now, show her.
> And Marilyn, you sing your part with Mum.

As Mum sang my part, I drifted off again thinking
> —that voice so sure,
> so strong, so out of my reach . . .
> Ah, listen. Marilyn's got that
> melody just right, doesn't she?
> Mum and she, such a lovely duet.

> Hear that, Dolores, isn't it pretty?
> We'll just have to practice more.

Why do I have to sing at all?
I asked, only so slightly
holding back the defiance.

Because I say so, and I'm the boss here.
Don't ever forget that.

What I say goes.
If I say sing, you will sing.

My eyes filled with tears, and my throat was on the
verge of a choke when Mum chimed in:
Alvin, let's forget this song for now.
Let's leave it for today.

There you go taking her part, again.
Those tears don't mean anything to me.
I'll let her go this time, but she will learn
to do it the way I want it, so don't think
you're getting your way here.

Good, I said to myself.
Theresa Brewer I'll never be.
The Andrew Sisters, no way.
No, not even Dinah Shore.
And Kate Smith?
Who really cares? Not me!
Fortunately the heat was off for the next few songs, as we
focused more on the dramatic, giving me a chance to breathe
as we mimed and mocked our way through "Thumbelina," and
"The Ugly Duckling."

There once was an ugly duckling
With feathers all stubby and brown,
And the other birds in so many words
Said: Quack!

Suzanne was perfectly serious as she tucked her three-and-
a-half year old arms up under themselves like the wings of
a duck, and waddled around obediently acting out our every
direction.

Suzanne's every activity was a balm to Dad's nerves—the
very nerves I so clearly irritated.

> *Get out*
> *Quack!*

I relished the words

> *Get out!*
> *Quack, quack!*

Suzanne quacked with intensity,
her pudgy face in a full frown
at our jeering voices.

> *Get out of town!*
> *And he went with a quack and*
> *a waddle and a quack*
> *in a flurry of Eiderdown.*

In a flurry of Eiderdown.
I loved that line.
What a sight—Sue waddling and quacking,
feathers flapping.
Her face appropriately somber,
yet bright with delight.
As the tone of the song's words
changed, mine did, too.

> *All through the winter time*
> *He hid himself away.*
> *Ashamed to show his face.*
> *Afraid of what others might say.*

Oh, the doubt the words described.

> *All through the winter*
> *in his lonely clump of weed*
> *'Til a flock of swans spied him there*
> *and very soon agreed.*

"You're a very fine swan, indeed."
Swan? Me a swan? Aw go on.

A part of me identified and wondered,
"Is it possible, surely there's something
I can do right, something that's mine."
Then, our last song—

> *Anywhere I wander. Anywhere I roam*
> *'Til I'm in the arms of my darling again*
> *My heart will find no home.*

Mum said:
   That's the best register for your voice, Dolores.

I winced inside, but didn't falter.

> *His voice was oh such a soft caress*
> *of love it gently told*
> *And in his smile was a tenderness*
> *I may never more behold.*

My longings at that moment exactly paralleled those of the song. I, if the truth be named, wanted so badly to sing beautifully, thinking if I could, maybe I would again receive the tenderness of Dad's smile, a tenderness I feared I might never see again.

— *Early Winter '55* —

The singing practice sessions did come to an end when Dad was persuaded by a friend to try a new venture in sales. With his real estate business plodding and slow, he was vulnerable to Tom T's enthusiasm and the promise of fast money to be made out West—Edmonton specifically—selling industrial education programs to young men. "That's one godforsaken place in winter," Dad would finally conclude, but only after making what had to be a seriously ill-considered journey.

Mum recalls:
> They took two cars (Dad's Cadillac, of course)—towing one to
> save on gas.

"What?" I ask.

> Well, sure, they used to do things like that. They went via the
> States, passing through Chatham on their way to Detroit, and on
> to Chicago. They stopped in to see my parents. Pépère told me
> he cried when he saw them taking off like that.

Why, I wonder, did Dad even stop there on his way?
Forever going to the dry well to drink.

Mum caught, as it were, always between our Dad and her own. We
children the hemp in this never to be resolved tug-of-war.

But,
we had no definitions then, only the
allegiance that comes with blood.

We received word from Dad every few days by mail. The trip was
very difficult, and somewhere in the Dakotas they were even
marooned for several days in a motel.

Mum:
> Snowstorms made the roads impassable. They were lucky
> to have made it to shelter. Some people were found stranded,
> literally frozen to death in their cars. Happily, once in
> Edmonton, they were made welcome by T's in-laws, the
> McK's, an established, well-to-do family out there.

But,
Dad's letters began to give hints that
things weren't turning out quite as planned.

He wrote:
> *There's nothing to do but read.*
> *You can't imagine the cold. The*
> *wind is positively wicked. We're*
> *cooped up inside most of the days,*
> *and at night we try to talk to*
> *people about these courses but*
> *we're not selling a damn thing! It's*
> *hard for them to see the value in*
> *training by mail . . .*

> *I miss you all. I'm so very lonely.*

Always so successful in sales, he tried to tough it out, but endured the ordeal only four months.

One day, out of the blue we got a call:
> I'm on my way home.
> In fact, I'm already swingin' through
> Chicago, expect to be home tomorrow!

Eighteen hours later, he arrived.
Laughing, he said,
> "I didn't even stop for a coffee."

His joy was infectious, and I welcomed the vitality of his presence as he took me in his arms, his great, great arms.

> *Anywhere I wander, anywhere I roam*
> *His arms were warm as they welcomed me*
> *His eyes were fire bright*

> *And then I knew that my path must be*
> *Through the ever-haunted night.*

Mum recalls:
> When he got home, he was still trying to sell those courses, but he did no better in Toronto than he had in Edmonton, so I said to him, "I think I'd better go and see if I can find some employment."

*M*um had often talked about going back to teaching; she really loved that and was a natural teacher. Certainly with us she was always a tireless, infinitely patient helpmate when it came to our various school projects, and homework. But, getting a job teaching wasn't a simple apply-and-get affair. It would require time and effort she could ill-afford. With her education, training, and the fact that she was fully bilingual, she quickly did get a job beginning as a proofreader in the French section of Simpson Sears retail and catalogue advertising division.

She remembers:
      I started to work July 18, 1955.

Meanwhile Dad dreamt of making a million with a poem.
Edna Jaques did it, why not me?

Born in Collingwood in 1891 to a Capt. Charles Jaques, Edna grew up literally next door to Ma and though younger by a few years, she was a very dear childhood friend. When Edna's family left Collingwood to homestead in Saskatchewan, she and Ma kept up their friendship as pen pals for years. When Jaques' brother married Ma's younger sister – that was one more reason to stay close.

Ma, an ardent lover of verse, remembered every poem she'd ever read and loved to recite them. She was particularly fond of those written by Edna.

Of Edna Jaques, the 1965 edition of Canadian Literature in English says, "The Poet Laureate of the Home writes to the song her kettle sings."

114

— Collingwood, Ontario —

It was a little town that cradled me,
  Behind it rose blue hills to meet the sky,
And by its threshold lapped an inland sea
  Where little puffy boats went sailing by.

And I remember cool unhurried lanes
  Where bare brown feet went pattering up and down,
With old back yards and orchards in the sun
  Behind the stately houses of the town.

Gay playmates of a happy childhood land,
  Fences to walk and swaying trees to climb,
Old broken dishes set against a wall,
  And all the glowing kingdom that was mine.

New bread with flaky crusts and lots of jam
  Cookies with scalloped edges crisp and thin,
Gardens to dig for treasures in the sand
  Small creeks to wade and fish for minnows in.
Old ladies primly sitting on the lawn,
  Green tangled hedges growing wild and dense,
Old fashioned flowers nodding in the sun
  We peeked at them through knot-holes in the fence.

Ah dear enchanted land that gave us birth,
  Gave us her soil, her hidden ways to know,
Pathways to bear the imprint of our feet,
  Making us hers, wherever we might go.

Now, Edna—a successful semiretired poet and lecturer—had come back East, looked Ma up, and with that reunion, Dad and she became friends. She would be his balm in Gilead.

There were many threads of experience they held in common. She loved to tell stories and he loved to listen—stories of struggle, like the winter her husband left her and her infant daughter to fend for themselves in the desolate wilds of the Saskatchewan prairies. And of course there were the inspiring stories of her life as a poet. And most impressive to Dad was the fame Edna Jaques had achieved for "In Flanders Now." Written in 1918 in answer to Colonel McCrae's immortal poem, "In Flanders Now" was used at the unveiling of the Unknown Soldier in Washington, D.C. It was printed on a card with the Belgian National Anthem and sold in the U.S. by the Federation of Women's Clubs; a million dollars were raised and used for the restoration of the Louvain Library.

— *In Flanders Now* —

We have kept faith, ye Flanders' dead,
Sleep well beneath those poppies red
That mark your place.
The torch your dying hands did throw,
We've held it high before the foe,
And answered bitter blow for blow,
In Flanders' fields.
And where your heroes' blood was spilled,
The guns are now forever stilled
And silent grown.
There is no moaning of the slain,
There is no cry of tortured pain,
And blood will never flow again,
In Flanders' fields.
Forever holy in our sight
Shall be those crosses gleaming white,
That guard your sleep.
Rest you in peace, the task is done,
The fight you left us we have won,
And Peace on Earth has just begun,
In Flanders now.

The success of that poem became the model for a success Dad began to wish to achieve for himself. But that success would never happen and the pursuit of it would become just another battle line drawn in the sand between him and Mum.

❖ ❖ ❖ ❖

Autumn 1955

A new school year meant
getting something new to wear.
In our house that was almost always
something Mum made for us,
or we made for ourselves.

That year Mum
made me a beautiful soft cotton skirt.
It was a deliciously vivid shade of turquoise.

Now,
everyone knows, there are clothes
and there are clothes!
That skirt gave me a sense of power.
Not a muscular, masculine power.
No, a power wholly whimsical—
like dancing, whistling, singing.
The skirt had swing.
The skirt had flair.
With my white bobby socks, and
black and white saddle shoes,
I was in tune with a trend,
I was growing up.

It was a turning point in so many, many ways.
But who knew that then?
Not me. All I knew was:

    With Mum going to work I had a whole new set of
    household responsibilities. Was I a mother now?

    When she told me to expect a certain fact of life—
    menstruation, I was not thrilled to hear it.

    Dad was awarded membership in the Rideout
    Millionaire's Club, an acknowledgement of his selling
    more than a million dollars' worth of real estate in his
    two years with that broker.

We were proud. His spirits were buoyed.

We were relieved.

He painted his blue Cadillac
(rusted from the trip out West)
pink and white.
I found that embarrassing.

We got our first man teacher, Mr. Mills.
All the girls thought "he's cute."

And, the Brooklyn Dodgers were competing for the
World Series against the New York Yankees!
That was amazing!

*B*aseball became one of our favorite pastimes.

I was never really that interested,
or that serious about playing.
It was mainly a chance to yell and to scream,
to jump around.

Partly, I was trying hard to escape the changes
that were taking place in my twelve-year-old body.
I had the notion if
I laughed loudly enough,
talked incessantly, maybe
          it would just all go away,
          I could stop the process in its tracks.

Take my legs.
The sight of them could, if Dad's mood was such,
elicit an onslaught of verbal abuse.
"Get inside, cover up those legs!"

The message was without equivocation—hide!

So,
(getting back to baseball),
there I was crouched down waiting my turn to bat when
suddenly I caught sight of my legs.
Oh, no! Horror of horrors!
My play shorts had risen!
My thighs floated before my eyes like balloons.
The sight of my own legs frightened me.

No one should see!
According to Dad I was "fat," and and, I imagined, "ugly, too."
His words were fact!

    Hide!

Oh, gee, quick
jump up and down,
scream!
"Bring that girl home! Miss that ball!
Stay in the outfield, buddy!"
The shorts fell back below my knees.
Okay, okay, okay.
It was done, they were covered.
I hoped no one was looking.

Then there was the day Mum instructed me
on the facts of menstruation.
I listened, but didn't really comprehend.
Didn't really want to.
The idea of my body preparing for
the day I might want to have a baby was
nothing I ever cared to hear.

She suggested
       "It'll soon be necessary for you
        to begin wearing a bra—and girdle!"

Who? What? Me! Oh, no!

I received and filed this information
in the same part of my mind as the
hide imperative Dad issued about my legs.

Hide!

Shame now defined
my relationship to my body.
I walked with my hands in a gesture of prayer,
my forearms folded
to cross over and hide my tiny budding breasts.

Shame defined the embarrassment I felt
toward Dad painting his car pink.
Who did he think he was anyway, Elvis Presley!

Hide!
I wanted to escape sexual identity altogether.

Hide!
Yes, Hide!

The shame and the fear propelled me.
I had spark, I had verve,
I was quick and outspoken.
Grades seven and eight would be two
of my most glorious school years.

Though popular with my classmates,
teachers found me a contradiction—
smart but impossible to control.

No doubt about it, I was arrogant, rebellious.
Hey, what do you mean,
I can hear the lesson you're teaching
and talk to Elizabeth, too!
Didn't I get mostly A's last term!

I poured my percolating energies into
a mixture of mischief-making,
and academic competition,

120

enjoying anything that gave me the
opportunity to stand up and perform —
poetry recitations, public speaking, and
Current Events—activities that paralleled
Dad's more ardent enthusiasms of the moment.
I parroted many of his passionate opinions
in my own presentations.

Those were heady days for Canada—
what with Lester B. Pearson
giving us a seat at the international table.
He was my "ideal Canadian."
Dad said Pearson was
"a mediator—he brings warring parties together."

Beyond our borders,
the U.S./Soviet conflict was heating up
with the U.S. hurling its threats of
"massive retaliation" and "nuclear attack."
Leaflets came in the mail
warning of Communism and the Cold War.

All this had Dad very agitated.
Middle East turmoil in particular affected him:

as tensions there intensified, his emotional temperatures rose.

He was regularly sending letters, poems to heads of state—
Prime Minister Anthony Eden, President Nasser and others,
expressing his concerns, his hopes for peace.

— POEM OF THE NATIONS —

Why seek we now
Odd blending still
With doubt and some duress
We share the task
To unravel here
The worldly needs that bless.
Languages goods abundant stored
Color cultures skills possessed
Must work at LOVE
Bind ourselves
To ends
We know will rest.
The best of ends
Are served for need
Goods far strewn all
Serve not for greed
Or thoughts that cleave
Or creeds with ends of gall.
Where lies the truth
It is benign
Self-seeking not its end.
Rejoices not in victory
Searches
Folds and tends.
This may grow great
That may turn small
Opposites not by chance
Support through each the pedestals
That all
May all enhance.
Truth moving still
Is undenied
Diffuse amid us kind
"CHILD OF FAITH" quoth HE
MY HEIRS SHALL BE
BIND EACH YOUR HEART IN MINE.

Alvin John Brandon.

NOON

He couldn't sleep for thinking of world affairs.

Mum disparaged Dad's
nascent activities as a "man of letters" and
her failure to support him
fed his deepening paranoia,
leading to ever more frequent arguments.

She, he said,
was to blame
for his life's stagnation.

Sometimes I think he might've been right.
He couldn't sleep for thinking of world affairs.

Mum disparaged Dad's
nascent activities as a "man of letters" and
her failure to support him
fed his deepening paranoia,

She was quick to throw her pail of cold water
on his hot ideas. Maybe they'd have been happier
apart. Maybe Dad would've been less angry
if he hadn't always been so constantly opposed.

One day my teacher, Mr. Mills, posed the question,
"Do any of you ever feel ashamed of your parents?"

What a question!

I was confronted with an idea I'd never, ever considered.

The whole class waited
in a state of stunned silence
for someone to respond. Finally,
one girl slowly raised her hand.
Tears fell from her dark brown eyes,
her head hung low as
she stammered the words,

Yes, I'm ashamed of my father.
He drinks a lot.
He makes me feel I don't want to know him.
He fights with my mother on the street
Calls her bad names for all the neighbors to hear.

I thought
My Dad doesn't drink, but
I know what she means.

I know
I know
I know

Shame
Shame is a spider
She weaves a web in my throat

Shame is a scream in the dark
Shame is a shattering of glass,
a head smashed through
Shame is Mum's black eye in the morning

Shame is asking for help

I don't remember ever talking about this with anyone.

Mum didn't talk about it,
not one of us did.

I know some of the neighbors did hear
Dad's voice, and the screams
that came with the fighting at our house.
I thought I could tell by the way they'd
ask, "How is your Mum, how is your Dad?"
There was a certain sorry look in their eyes.
I'd just say
"They're fine."
And hold my head high.

Mum says:
>   "In those days, some people thought I must be
>   to blame, said I must have done something to
>   deserve it."

I know there were chums of Dad's who knew.
I could tell by the way they'd
pat Mum on the back tenderly, knowingly.
She was always treated quite sweetly by his friends.
(Dad wasn't above insulting her in front of them
and some were brave enough to come to her defense.
I liked that.)

It would be a long long time before I could admit
the shame I felt in relation to my Dad.

Like Mum
I wanted just
to love him
to hold on
to forgive him his trespasses.

Yes, I hated the bully in him
and I felt really angry a lot of the time
but I also felt sad, so, so sad.
I told myself
>   The problem's bigger than he is.
>   He's not a bad man.
>   God is to blame.

Suzanne, (second from left) with playmates 1956.

Winter 1956

The rhythms of Mum's workday
set the pattern of our lives.

Due at the office by 8:00 a.m., she was
up at 5:30 a.m.
Marilyn, Suzanne and I
got up just as she was leaving.
Dad was there to help us with breakfast.

Suzanne, just shy of kindergarten age,
spent her days with our next door neighbor.
We'd pick Sue up around 4:00 p.m.
on our way in from school.

With Mum working
Marilyn and I had
many more household chores.

There were
  beds to make,
  morning dishes to do,
  and supper to prepare
  before Mum got home at 6:30 p.m.

I, as the eldest,
was held somewhat more accountable for
the smooth running of this operation.

With Dad now acting more and more like his own father,
I knew and feared the terrible consequences
I'd suffer if things weren't done right or on time.

Sometimes Marilyn and Suzanne
moved too slowly for me.
"You're making me late!"
I cried. Then, in a panic, imagining Dad,
and a possible blow to the head,

I scolded, and urged:
                Come on we've got to move faster!

They in turn called me "bossy."
               I am not!
               I am not!
               I am not!

I cried in despair.

Dad's going to be mad!
It'll be me who takes the blame.
And, I am not your mother!

               Not your mother!
               Not your mother!
               No, never, never, not me!

Mum arrived home each day
    with the latest episode in office gossip, and
    Simpson Sears quickly
    became the main conversation piece
    at our supper table. Some days
    we'd have fun laughing at Mum's descriptions,
    Dad making jokes.

    Over the years
    we'd get to know more about the people Mum worked with,
    people we'd never meet,
    than we ever knew about neighbors
    and relatives we saw all the time.

    But the most special thing about Mum's job
    was the Bargain Center.
    Considering she made, before taxes,
    $40 a week,
    and Dad's income was increasingly erratic,
    it is easy now
    for me to understand the enthusiasm
    she felt for every cent saved on a purchase made there.

NOON

Every day after lunch
(a lunch she packed and carried from home),
she'd scour the little Sears' Employees Only store
where they displayed catalogue clearance items.

Whatever we needed—
pajamas,
flannel-lined blue jeans,
coats and hats, mittens,
sweaters and scarves—
she found it there.

Every appliance bought thereafter
also came from Sears.
With her 10% discount,
she made a dollar stretch
from earth to the moon.
Like most kids, though,
we didn't always appreciate
the hardships she endured
to feed and clothe us,
and on occasion we expressed
a haughty contempt for
"that bargain center stuff."

At a recent family Christmas, talk
turned unexpectedly to this time,
and Mum revealed:
> I never handled any of our finances. Oh, no. I
> never even saw the bank book. Every payday I
> handed my check over to Alvin, and he'd give me
> an allowance. I barely had enough money to get
> back and forth to work. Some days I couldn't even
> afford a 10¢ cup of tea in the cafeteria.

The freedom Mum won working
came with a whole new kind of bondage.

Words like
        martyr,
        castrator,
        soul-destroyer
                larded Dad's vocabulary in
                arguments from then on.

Mum's success outside the home stirred
the bile of his deepest insecurities and
he never hesitated to remind her:

        Just because you're bringing in a few dollars
        doesn't make you better than me. You'll never
        make the kind of money I made. You'll never do
        what I've done. I bought this house with the
        money I earned, I own it.

Spring 1956

Dad bought a piece of property in Victoria Harbor
from Tom T's father, himself a contractor.
It had been a dream of Dad's to build a house with his own hands;
his father had done so, and his grandfathers before him.
He had the idea that maybe
he could make a living building cottages for sale.
This one served as an experiment.

Mum remembers:
> When the snow melted in April, Dad got started.
> As the weather warmed he'd stay up there all
> week, living in a tent, working during the days,
> coming home on weekends. It was actually thera-
> peutic; he liked camping, being outside.
>
> One day he went into town for a haircut, only to
> find a sign on the door—"Gone Fishing." He liked
> that. It was so different from the hectic pace he'd
> been keeping in Toronto.
>
> With help from a carpenter living in Victoria
> Harbor, he finished by late summer. We spent at
> least one week there in August, and a few week-
> ends, too. Boy was it primitive! I don't think we
> even had a door on the outhouse.

Outhouse?
(I laugh)
> Well, he didn't want to put a whole lot of money
> into it, not knowing for sure how fast it would
> sell. So, no, there was no indoor plumbing, just
> the outhouse. It faced the valley in back. You
> could sit there and see rabbits running by, birds
> flying past.

Mutual laughter
> He didn't dig a well either. We had to carry our
> water from the one across the road.

Reminiscent of
Long Branch?
> Oh boy, even worse! The Victoria Harbor cottage
> was very well built, very sturdy, but it was a shell
> only. There was a room designated for a bath-
> room, but Dad never installed it. Eventually he did
> put a door on the outhouse.

Wasn't that a bit
hard on you, working
all week, then going
there to rough it like
that?
> Oh, Dad thought it would be relaxing, thought I
> needed a change weekends, thought I'd be home
> washing walls, or something.

(Laughter)
Mum always was a little
obsessive with cleaning.

> Anyway, he'd pick me up right there at Sears'
> door on Fridays, and we'd go to the cottage.

Did you find
it relaxing?
> (Laughter.)
> Oh, I don't know. There were no beds—just old
> mattresses on the floor. There was no insulation,
> of course, so it could get pretty cold at night.
> We'd throw the tent on top of us.

What were you
cooking on?
> A hot-plate.

Oh, God! That again!
Back to ground zero!

Today,
Mum tries to gloss over the pain, but
I remember
> she wasn't at all thrilled with these weekends.
> She never liked camping or anything resembling it.
> She liked the conveniences of her suburban home.

Expressing displeasure, however,
provoked anger in Dad. She was
> *the bad one,*
> *the thorn in his side,*
> *the saboteur of his dreams.*

The closest she'll come
now to talking about
this side of things
is to say:
> None of us liked cottage life. We went there,
> though, for at least three summers. Dad finally
> sold it to a man who was retiring, wanted to live a
> simple life. He bought it and finished it.

Did Dad make a profit?

> Yes, but not enough to encourage him to build
> another one. He decided it was not a business to
> get into.

Nevertheless, the building bug had hold,
and Dad set about fixing
the basement at home.

Mum supported this wholeheartedly.
He did a wonderful job.

When the work was done,
they celebrated with a big party.
About fifty people came.

They ate while they watched and cheered
the Grey Cup Final, then
sang and danced the night away.

Dad was in his element.
He had a new persona for the occasion — the one-man band.
He played two instruments at once: chords on the guitar,
a harmonica attached to a prop 'round his neck.

He wore gag-oriented rubber costume accessories —
a big nose, and a pair of huge floppy bare feet —
to recite one of his more humorous poems:

— *The Panel Show* —

You are Irish
Yes?
NO
To hell with that
Then you are English.
Well, no
A little fat.
You're Scots
I know
You have a goat?
Heck, no
That's Greek
And a petticoat.

Try. Guess again.
There is lots of whys.
It's hard to guess
Unless one surmise.
Maybe you're a Yank
You like the buck?

No?
Then maybe you're
Even
Jack Canuck.

NOON

Come on panel.
I know now
Don't like to jeer
But you're French
You've got cattle
Your beef
I hear.

Aw, well now
Let's start anew
I can't guess more
Give us a clue.
Time's up
Bell's gone
I'll let you in.
I'm one of them thar
Bi-Canadians

Alvin John Brandon.

Late Summer 1956

I turned thirteen—a bona fide teenager.

Mr. Woods, my teacher, was young,
not long out of school himself.
He loved the poetry of Robert Service and
encouraged us to recite the rhythmic verses aloud.

There are strange things done in the midnight sun
By the men who moil for gold

One day, out of the blue, he called me
"Dolly."
The nickname took hold, everyone adopted it.
At first I liked it, then I didn't.
I had mixed feelings about it, like
I had mixed feelings about everything.

"Dolly"—
Was this new name an honor or a tease?
Did I remind him of a dog?
Was I just another Raggedy Ann?
Or did he just like the sound of the word?

Then, too, it could be
he, like Dad,
didn't like my name.

I heard Dad say so in fights with Mum,
fights in which he
relentlessly replayed traumas of their early days,
like the time he was denied attendance
at my Baptism in the Roman Catholic Church.
My name was an ever-present reminder.

He ranted, and blamed Mum:
    I was nothing, I was nobody to them!
    You, you let it happen. You chose her
    name, I didn't. Dolores, just another

name for your goddamned Virgin Mary.
You worshippers of false idols.

Who the hell needs an intercessor anyway?
In my book, you either talk to God directly,
or not at all!

So "Dolly" it was, and
the name gave me wings,
an identity separate from the one defining me at home.
That year I soared
to the top of the class in almost everything.
At Christmas I was the girl my classmates selected
to present a basket of food and gifts
to a needy family in the neighborhood.
The boy they chose was an Elvis look-a-like!

But my success and popularity at school
didn't save me at home.
It provided no protection from Dad.

One weekday afternoon that winter,
I decided to go to the movies
with a girlfriend, Sandra, after school.
I didn't ask permission, didn't tell my sisters,
I just went.

The feature was "Picnic"—
and fairly irrelevant, inasmuch as
our interest was boys!

We divided our time between
cruising the aisles and buying things to eat
as a means to getting ourselves seen.
Taking our cues from the love scenes we saw on
the screen, we were eager to experience the same
pleasures the beautiful movie stars did.

Twinkling footlights guided us into pitch-dark
theater rows—perfect indoor alleyways for sexual
experimentation.

We allowed ourselves to be kissed, yes
kissed and fondled by perfect strangers,
boys we'd never before seen!
When I did get home that day,
it was after seven,
already dark.

As I opened the back door,
Mum and Dad, together,
lunged toward me.
Dad first,
knocking me to the floor, demanded
"Where have you been?"
"At the movies," I stammered.
Kicking me, he yelled
"You tramp. Who were you with?"
"Sandra," I whispered.
"Who's she? Some boy-crazy slut?"
And he kicked me again.

I pee'd on myself.

Shame is running scared along a dark road

Mum urged him on:
"You had us worried half sick.
Why didn't you ask, tell us you were going?"
"Cuz she's a no good tramp,"
Dad answered, and grabbed me by the arm.
"Get up, get in here," he yelled.

Dead weight, barely able to move,
I lay cowering, crying in the tiny back vestibule,
expecting any moment to be
thrown down the stairs.
"Get up," he repeated, and yanked me to my feet.

Shame walks across my face,
dances in the recesses of my eyes

NOON

I managed to stand.
He shoved me into the kitchen.
Mum backed up so I could pass.
My sisters were nowhere to be seen.
I went directly to my room.

I remember
　A song
　　A voice
　　　A tongue
　　　　A fragment
　　　　　(Micaela's song from "Carmen"):

　　　　　　　Je dis, que rien ne m'épouvante
　　　　　　　Je dis, hélas! Que je réponds de moi;
　　　　　　　Mais j'ai beau faire la vaillante, Au fond du
　　　　　　　coeur je meurs d'effroi!

I say nothing
is afflicting me
I can vouch for myself
I try to be brave
but I am dying of fright.

　　Seule en ce lieu sauvage, Toute seule j'ai peur . . .

Alone in this wild place,
all alone, I am afraid.

There is no heavenly Father
listening to my prayers!

I thought of Harold, the boy
I'd really wanted to meet at the movies,
the boy who didn't show up, never would.

　　Shame is feeling you're never good enough

Mum and Dad continued to spew forth:
What kind of girl can this Sandra be?
What kind of family's she from?

139

Did her parents know where she was?
Did she call home before going?
We were on the verge of calling the police.
You know what they call girls who are out alone at night?
Whores, that's what.

I asked myself:
    What's a slut, what's a whore anyway?
    Sandra, poor girl, she's not a close friend,
    just someone I know.

Didn't he always say
"and a little child shall lead them."

From this day on it became
"I can scorn, and let her go."

❖ ❖ ❖ ❖

When I began to menstruate sometime that year,
I didn't say a word.
The first time blood flowed,
I took out the little supply of
sanitary paraphernalia Mum had given me
the day she'd explained
this particular fact of life.

Darn, this thin elastic belt
pinching my skin.
Oh yuk, why this
awkward wad
suspended between my legs?

Fearing a mishap,
I walked pinching my thighs together slightly,
ready to squeeze them closed
should this diaper-like intrusion slip out of place.

140

Unwilling to accept
"my monthly visitor" as "friend,"
I decided to make my own
more streamlined sanitary pads
with Kleenex and safety pins!
They weren't exactly models of efficiency.

Nevertheless, when Mum asked
about the blood stains
she found on my laundry now and then,
I denied any knowledge.

I never officially told her. And when
girlfriends talked of menstruation,
proud to have it as an excuse not to go swimming,
I lied, saying, "Not me, no. I do not bleed."
No way was I bragging to anyone that I was becoming a
woman.

> *Shame lives in the loins.*
> *Shame is blood on white cotton panties.*

*7*hat spring
I won the public speaking contest
with a speech describing the Calgary Stampede—
taken almost verbatim from *The Reader's Digest*.
I described the cowboy's lasso tricks with gusto and glee.
I lived vicariously in vivid descriptions of bucking broncos.
You'd think I'd actually been to a rodeo, but no,
I was merely exercising my ability to imagine
things I'd never seen,
getting a glimpse of the actress I aspired to be.

That June I was selected Valedictorian.
For the occasion Mum helped me make a white dress—
a soft satin-finished cotton—it
had a simple boat neck at the front
dropping to a V in back,
a full mid-calf length skirt.

We accessorized the dress
with a length of lemon yellow dotted swiss organdy
I tied around my waist
to make a butterfly bow at the back.
I got my first pair of pumps—also white,
to be worn with white nylons.
Wanting to look my very best,
I decided to have my hair done professionally.
The style I imagined—a bustle:
a cluster of curls to be arranged at the back of my neck.
It was a hairstyle Mum wore
when she was younger and
I was just a little girl.
I'd always loved it,
she looked so elegant and glamorous—
maybe I would, too.

Graduation day arrived;
it was exceedingly hot and humid.

In the hours between
getting my hair done in the morning
and the ceremony that evening,
every curl in the bustle had uncurled.
I was left with a stringy straight pony tail.

Tears streamed down my face.

Without Mum's help
I might not have gone on.
But she held me close,
encouraged me, saying,
        Don't worry, my dear, sweet girl.
        With those big brown eyes
        you're just the girl I
        dreamed I would have.
        You'll do well.
        Just wait and see.

Like a veteran performer
I did do her proud:
        Your voice and bearing oh my!
        You put me in mind of the Queen
        of England.

I guess I knew a few
things about saying goodbye.

❖ ❖ ❖ ❖

As surely as the hands of a clock
keep time beneath a face of glass,
I passed from puberty to adolescence
without any obvious loss.
But as surely as noon opposes midnight,
I was not the same girl.

By sixteen I was a self-styled beatnik.
With white lipstick,
eyes heavily outlined in black pencil,
back-combed hair, and black stockings,
I was staking out an identity as outsider.
My high school yearbooks betray
the anguished identity battles of those years:
where there ought be five photos—
one for each school year—
there's only one.
Not because my picture wasn't taken,
no, nothing that benign.

The pictures have been surgically removed,
mutilated by none other than my own hand!

In the ninth grade class photo
where I should be seen sitting there's a hole.
I literally scissored myself out.

The tenth grade class photo must have
met my sadist's approval because
it remains undisturbed.
That picture is black and white, but
I know for certain the corduroy jumper
I made for myself was red—
a lovely clear tulip red.
Of the eleventh grade image all that remains
are scratches—

I viciously attacked my face and eyes with a pen.
By the twelfth grade,
I'm simply willfully absent.

144

I don't have the yearbook for the thirteenth grade, but
I well remember the graduation day photo.
My hair was in a fashionable beehive,
and I no longer wore glasses.
I had a presence, an intensity, a well-earned
pride about me, a pride I inherited from my
mother and my grandmothers.
I remember giving that photo to "my first true love,"
someone I'd meet my first year at Western University.
Comparing me to my classmates, he said:

> "Wow, you look like a star;
> you make the others look like
> mere schoolgirls."

Little wonder that fellow still holds a place dear in my heart.

❖ ❖ ❖ ❖

Give me the heat
And the dust of man
where I
Can be a light
all is not darkness
some is day
and daylight
Follows night

Give me a heart
Part worn with care
Some grief some pleasure
                    there
and I will live
As my father lived
For there
Was some despair

Alvin John Brandon.

146

Night

Summer 1960

*B*y summer 1960, Dad's psychosis was full-blown.

Whom God wishes to destroy, he first makes mad.

His rhythms quickened,
He was up night and day,
favored clothing in red.

Moving himself into the garage,
he hung a karate chart on the wall,
a punching bag from the beams,
his real estate broker's sign from the door.

And a man's foes shall be they of his own household.

Bedroom and kitchen were his rings of battle:
stove steaming rage,
pots of scorched dreams,
bread of Christ,
tables of troubled trust.
It was "a long day's journey . . ."

Keep silence now for singing time is over.

We were flotsam whirling in a vortex.
Five feet, ten inches tall—
a two hundred and twenty-five pound volcano
spewing verbal lava.
We were his "ball and chain, lead in his feet,
bitches, bloodsuckers, parasites,
living off the fat of (his) land."

He loathed the sight of my body—
my thighs "mustn't be seen."
I was "not to wear shorts, ever after"
in the heat of an August afternoon.

149

The food I was ordered to cook, then serve him,
though "swill not fit for a pig,"
he downed like there was no tomorrow.

His jaw cracked on the teeth of his anger
and he scolded that I was "eating too fast."

Unwilling to be cast as his shadow
I talked back, screaming, "I hate you, you liar!"

Daring to look him in the eye as I did so,
I watched for the pain my words caused.
He was stunned momentarily, and I saw it,
but he quickly regrouped and rebounded.
Mum tried to put a stop to "this nonsense"
only to stir an all-out rampage.
His fists rose to hit her—
fed up now, I threw myself into his path,
absorbing the blows meant for her.

Marilyn and Suzanne took refuge
in the bedroom they shared.

> Years later Marilyn told me she was hiding
> in the closet praying none of us would die.

Summer decayed into autumn,
help was nowhere to be found.
Our family doctor turned a deaf ear.
Mum's only defense—"We have to endure.
This is my cross to bear."

One night the battle got bloody.
I'm no longer in touch with the cause,
but I recall very clearly how
he cornered and beat me in the rec room,
his fist making contact with my nose.
I fell to the floor curling in on myself
like a crib child.
Mum ran to the phone calling "POLICE."
Dad, hearing her plea, ran after, threatening revenge.

150

NIGHT

Believing he was capable of homicide,
we dashed from the house to the lawn.
    Mercifully, the police arrived quickly,
    but our ordeal had only begun.
    Mum described to the officers what had happened,
    our terror. They went to the door seeking Dad.
    When he appeared I saw his skin weeping,
    and his eyes, so very afraid.
    But he mustered a calmness, a reason,
    and the police accepted him at his word.
    "It's only a family quarrel," they told us.
    "He'll cool off. Now, go on back inside."
    Mum refused this analysis and solution:

    "He's sick, can't you tell?
    Please help, get him mental health care."
    "We can't," they responded,
    "You need two doctors to sign."
    "Our lives are in danger," I stammered.
    "My nose—I think it may be broken."
    One officer said—"We'll take you
    to the hospital to check, if you like.
    And, if you press charges, we'll
    lock him up overnight."
    "Oh, no, he's no criminal!
    He's my Dad. I could never do that."
    "Well, that's all we can do. I'm sorry."

    "Okay, take us to the hospital in the Queensway,"
    Mum said, "And my two other girls, would you
    drop them at my sister-in-law's?
    She lives on the way."
    They consented. We left
    Dad alone with the house.

    Glancing back through the cruise car window
    the red brick bungalow smoked like a crater—
    the cool white trim 'round the windows and door
    flickered an innocence we were intent to preserve.

151

The police stopped first at Aunt Margaret's—
there Mum recounted our plight. She asked
if Marilyn and Suzanne could stay.
Uncle Hubert wasn't too eager to help, but
saw he hadn't much choice—so relented.

At the hospital a doctor determined
"It's nothing too serious.
Your nose—just cracked. Should heal on its own
without noticeable displacement.
For now, here's an ice pack. And,
see those stretchers in the hall?
You two can sleep there for a few hours."

Next morning, cousin Bill Lee came to get us.
We went back to Aunt Margaret's, and from there
Mum called the Minister of the United Church we attended.
He agreed to meet with her at his office where,
hearing her tell of the ordeal,
he decided to get us some help.
That very day he paid Dad a visit and
saw for himself what Mum said was so.
The Reverend, well,
he was an eloquent man of great influence, so
with a minimum of effort,
he secured the signatures of two doctors—
our own and another he knew.
He even got Dad to agree to go with him
"For a ride." The destination?
(Undisclosed to Dad)
Ontario Hospital.

It was the saddest day of our lives.
Another salesman dying.

   Nobody dast blame this man.

❖ ❖ ❖ ❖

*M*um, never one to ask for much help,
did call her parents and sisters that day,
letting them know what she'd had to do.

Aunt Julienne came to be with us that very weekend.
Suzanne, Dad's Echo, cracked under the strain.
She had a seizure—the first in her nine young years.
Aunt Julienne was a public health nurse; she
knew just what to do.
We'd have been helpless without her.

For now though, we were at the outset
of the long, long journey into Dad's goodnight.

Mum remembers:

> Aunt Margaret and Uncle Hubert didn't want anything to do
> with us after that. The whole Collingwood gang stayed
> away. They were afraid. My parents knew only that Dad
> was being hospitalized, they didn't know exactly what for.
> They didn't know I'd come near death many times, they
> didn't know you girls had been injured. Julienne didn't
> know, Glorianna didn't know. Dad's sisters didn't know.
> My family wrote Dad a few letters during the time he was
> away to lend him support, let him know he wasn't
> forgotten:

Dear Alvin:

*If we were closer, I would send you a piece of apple pie once in a
while. We have a lot of juicy windfall McIntosh apples. We often
think of you, and pray that you will be well again soon. We know
that you will be well again because you are so ambitious, and a
good boy. We will write again.*

From Treflé and Eulalie

Mum continues:
>Really, though, I fought the battle on my own.
>You children were my only support, my only consolation.
>Outside of you, I didn't have anyone.
>For weeks after Dad was committed, I wasn't allowed to see
>him. He was very angry, very bitter with me.
>He never did forgive me for putting him there.
>That first time, though, the doctors and nurses had to spend
>quite some time observing him, figuring out what exactly was
>wrong. Until they could calm him down, they thought it better
>that he not see me. I had to go there every week,
>though, to answer all kinds of personal questions.
>They never did speak to you children.

With Dad away
life got back to its normal routine.
We girls were kept busy with schoolwork,
maintaining our grades above average.
I was invited to join the collegiate sorority,
I'd a boyfriend or two—always very nice boys.
We enjoyed being in the orchestra at assemblies
wearing our new navy tunics, white blouses, black hose.
Marilyn excelled on her oboe. Me,
I never quite did keep the right time on my flute.
Instead, I just kibitzed my way through.

Mum said her job was a "godsend."
It kept her mind off her cares.
Suzanne, already the mother and teacher
she eventually grew up to become,
gathered the neighborhood towheads around her,
organizing their games and playschool drills.

Dad was gone several months before he
eventually got weekends at home; then,
it was a bittersweet reconciliation,
for the man we welcomed and called Daddy
was quite different from the man we had known.
His fine body was weaker, sedated,
his bright eyes told of things he couldn't share,

he was ever so grateful to be with us, but sad,
knowing the pass was just for two days.
Come Sunday he would leave us again.

One Friday Mum went to get him.
He'd just had a shock treatment, and
wouldn't be allowed to come home. But Dad
hadn't been told of the decision and
was eagerly awaiting her call. She
didn't know the situation yet either
and approached the door—as she did always.
He saw her through the glass, darkly
and ran to her outreaching arms.
The custodian rushed to restrain him.
A doctor informed Mum of the need
to withdraw the weekend privilege.

Dad was confused, didn't understand,
only knew he wanted out of there,
wanted to sleep in his very own bed,
feel the arms of his sweetheart,
taste the favorite foods she had made.
But no, that day it couldn't happen.
Poor baby man crying,
Crying so hard to be freed.

The six months Dad was gone passed relatively quickly.
When he finally came home for good
we were all glad, hoping the worst was in the past.
But it didn't quite happen that way.
Largactil, the medication they gave him,
resolved little—
only managed to keep him down.
His life was a mental purgatory.
A glazed faraway look took root in his eyes.

I prayed for miraculous powers
with which to erase his pain.

❖ ❖ ❖ ❖

— *Fall '61* —

It was my last high school year—
a difficult year at best.
Facing tough provincial exams,
I was under tremendous strain.
I had a nasty case of constipation;
it lasted the entire year.
We tried everything—laxatives, castor oil, mineral oil;
nothing worked. My skin broke out in despair.
I missed quite a few days of school.
When I did attend, feeling ashamed and ugly,
I sat faced rigidly forward, my hands cupped over
my speckled cheeks hoping no one would see,
trying to hide.

— *Late Spring '62* —

Seeing me go through a period of exam-related stress,
out of the blue Dad brought me a six-pack of port.
"Drink one of these," he said, "to calm your nerves."
We all laughed. There was a sweetness
in more than one chamber of his heart.
His better self knew we loved him—
knew we were the best friends he'd ever have.

June—I passed everything.
Not brilliantly—I never was that,
but good enough for university.
I chose Western, in London, Ontario.
It gave me a chance to leave home,
to follow in the steps of my mother, I suppose—
she'd gone there for summer courses in music
when she was the same age.

I took out a loan for tuition,
using money I'd made working that summer
for books and clothes.
Mum and Dad drove me up to London where
together we found a place where I would board.

It was a small, crowded family home—
not quite as anonymous as I needed. So,
a week or two later I found another
more suitable place where I shared
a room with an out-of-town girl
who went home every weekend,
leaving me with time to myself.

Mum sent me thirteen dollars a week—
six paid for the room with breakfast,
and seven gave me a dollar a day for my other meals.
(I practically lived on hot dogs and soup.)
Not knowing a soul when I first got there,
I threw myself into a social whirl, and
got myself nominated, then elected
Vice President of the Freshman class!
(In those days, only a boy could be President!)

I had boyfriends galore
(who helped feed me).
Despite my landlady's jealous suspicions,
my popularity was all pretty innocent,
my sexual impulses being
entirely sensible, as it were.

❖ ❖ ❖ ❖

*B*eing away freed up my room at home, and
sometime that winter Dad, trying to compensate
for his inability to provide, decided to offer it up
for board. The roomer—Uncle Frank Giffen's brother,
Bob. He was a bit of a hobo. As such he walked
into the soft spot in Dad's heart, and
of that time Dad even composed a poem:

> *Robust round*
> *A little shy*
> *. . .*

It was far from an ideal situation.

> *He rose at six*
> *Each and every day*
> *His job attend*
> *He earned his pay*

Drove a truck, I think.

> *He tried his best*
> *To please and more*
> *But one unfailing*
> > *Conqueror*

Bob enjoyed his cheap whiskey
and chain-smoked Lucky Strikes.

> *At four sometimes*
> *From to the door*
> *A little late*
> *Just had one more.*

> *No supper me*
> *I'll skip this one*
> *To rest would he*
> *He would be done.*

Bob was a sweet guy, but his hygiene wasn't charming—
the house took on the smell of his bad habits, and
Mum wasn't too happy washing his clothes!
When she found a cigarette burn or two 'round his room
Mum fretted, "He'll fall asleep with a lighted cigarette—
all we need is for the house to burn down thanks to him!"

Dad asked:
>   *Did this?*
>   *He said not I.*
>
>   . . .
>
>   *He left nor said*
>   *To whence he bore*
>   *We haven't seen*
>   *Since left the door.*

Bob just up and disappeared.

Mum's fears were borne out
a few years later when
a front page news story reported
Bob was one of two found dead
in a fire at Queen Elizabeth Hospital.
He was a patient there. Seems he
wandered off his Ward to visit
a woman in Intensive Care.
She was on oxygen. He lit a cigarette.
She and he, the whole room,
all blew to smithereens!

Mum says:
That could have been us!

❖ ❖ ❖ ❖

— *Spring '63* —

Dad stopped taking his medication.
By early summer he

> *. . . felt younger, lighter, happier in body . . . conscious of a heady recklessness, a current of disordered sensual images running like a millrace in (his) fancy, a solution of the bonds of obligation, an unknown but not an innocent freedom of the soul.*

The manic desires to construct
reemerged. He took off for
Collingwood where
Mum says:

> He made a real nuisance of himself: decided to install a toilet in Ma's hallway upstairs.

And, he was furiously writing poetry
dreaming of fortune and fame:

— *The Soldier* —

> *Oh, Lymph of life*
> *Benign unknown*
> *Gambols plays it turns*
> *In childhood free*
> *It lives within*
> *Blythe spirit*
> *So it burns*
>
> *In fields of grief*
> *A soldier strays*
> *Be brave Yea carry on*
> *He sees the slain*
> *The homeless waif*
> *His thoughts come as the dawn*
> *What for this fight*
> *Can it be that man*
> *Unlearned, untaught, ignored*

NIGHT

Has wandered from the
Paths of love
Left greed yet unexplored

We'll be again
All will be well
Home, friends, a child beside
Quick stole
The sting of hate has pierced
A bursting heart has died.

Alvin John Brandon.

It's not that his poems weren't half good.
They all sprang from the heart. But,
they were written as the wave
crested in a grandiose fury.
And the call they put out for harmony stood
in stark contrast to the aggressive force
he asked us to indulge.

It was the difference between a summer storm and a
cyclone; one providing refreshing relief from the heat,
the other threatening total destruction.

As the psychosis once again deepened,
the writing became rave.
Seeking to heal
the split in his twin ram's head—
he obsessed on unresolved failures in his past:
family feuds, the army breakdown,
the loss of a woman he loved.
And the intransigence of the Roman Catholic Church
stuck as the sharpest craw in his throat.

The Book of Revelation was the source of his Truth:

> *Come hither; I will shew unto thee the judgment of the great*
> *whore that sitteth upon many waters: with whom the kings*

161

of the earth have committed fornication, and the inhabitants
of the earth have been made drunk . . .

Sadly, rave only fed rage; no solace was achieved.
Religion, language, nationality—these fueled
preliminary lightweight knockdown rounds
before the heavyweight bout began. Then,
he had gender envy in his corner, and
woman was the object of obscene scatologic verbiage:
menstrual blood, pregnancy, the life-giving force—
they were all lumped together with dirt, filth, and sin.

Who can bring a clean thing, out of an unclean? Not one.

Mum was the particular body he chose to attack,
inflicting bruises, black eyes, despite which,
and with which she went to work every day.

Marilyn and I, too, had to stay out of his way.
Tabu, the sultry fragrance we liked to wear,
and any errant, innocent girlish glance could
become a probable cause for offense.
Suzanne was the only child to lead him.

This second breakdown was a downward
spiraling for us all and it was no easier
than the previous time to get help.

The Reverend distanced himself.
Like most everyone else, he too, was afraid.
Said, he had nightmares last time,
lost sleep after getting Dad put away.
Although he'd paid Dad two or three visits
during that first hospital stay,
something had happened in the months since
Dad had come home.
Something none of us is clear on.

Mum says she thinks Dad embarrassed the Reverend
one night in a prayer meeting, pushing a cause.

NIGHT

For (his) roarings are poured out like water,
and the thing which (he) fears comes upon (him).

So, the Reverend made quite a point
one Sunday—reaching right past Dad
to shake another congregant's hand.

Dad was quite hurt, and frankly on this one,
I think he'd a right to his pride.

Knowing our lives were again in serious danger,
Mum called Ontario Hospital, asking them to assist.
They sent a virtual army—police, ambulance,
doctors, and straitjacket crew.
It was a three alarm medical ambush—
lights, sirens, action.
Seeing them approach, Dad tried to run.
He hissed and fought like a cat.
But it was really no use 'gainst this posse—
they soon had him down for the count.
We—Mum, Marilyn, Suzanne, and myself—
huddled outside in midsummer's moonlight
caught in a centripetal flow of guilt, shame and rage.
Our eyes wakened to mourning as they took Dad away.

We're not the first who with best meaning,
have incurr'd the worst.

We talked about leaving him this time,
Mum thought maybe she should, but
the doctor would've asked, "How can you?
He's a sick man. He needs all the support you can give."
And the social worker counseled, "You're not likely
to get very far, he'll come after you,
perhaps even stalk you on your job."

163

Today Mum says:
      There wasn't much help in those times.

Also Mum knew if she left him, the
law'd give her few rights to anything
she'd worked so hard to maintain.

So she said:
      We just have to stay, and hope God's listening
      to our prayers.

Sometimes she'd
even advise:
      If you girls ever decide to marry, choose a man
      who loves you more than you love him.

It's pretty astounding as I consider it today

what we can absorb into our daily routines.
How life goes on—
not just that the sun rises to shine,
or the rain drops,
and night inevitably falls, but
that we actually conduct full lives, like
Mum then, going to work each day no matter what.
Not only going but achieving, every year
rising up in the ranks of her job,
up from French proofreader, eventually to manage
the entire bilingual editorial staff.

Stopped only by gender, for those were the days
women hit the ceiling hard and fast.
No glass ceiling, then, oh, no!
That ceiling was entirely visible, and very solid.
The "big boss,"
as Mum referred to some of her superiors,
was always a man.

164

NIGHT

I remember myself as a teenager,
preparing for a date only
minutes after one of Dad's outbursts—
dressing up, greeting my boyfriend,
looking radiant, even serene.
Yes, life went on.

Only much later would I know the toll it all took.
Only in my twenties would I realize
how much I feared men in positions of authority,
how conflicted, how afraid
I was to ask for anything I really wanted,
afraid I'd be rejected, hit in the head.
I, who without a minute's hesitation
had so often thrown myself bodily
in the path of Dad's rage, seeking to protect Mum,
to put an end to the violence.

As hard as our lives were,
I personally accept Mum's decision to stay.
I never disparage or disown this aspect of my root.

I may always fight to sublimate a wellsprung anger—
anger built up to resist, to rail against, to defend—
but I do not blame, and I am not bitter.

❖ ❖ ❖ ❖

Alvin Brandon, with a fellow patient, after graduating
classes of the Adult Retraining Centre, April 1963.

NIGHT

$\mathcal{D}$ad was away six weeks the second time.

I sometimes visited him at the hospital.
A benign, quiet loneliness greeted me at the iron gate
behind which rugged old brown Victorian brick
facilities stood solemn and sentinel.
The pale grey cement walkways wound to locked doors.
Black wire window grates frowned security.

I wanted so much for someone to explain,
help me understand. No one did.
The doctors and social workers were cordial,
but no one invited any substantive dialogue.
With a studied neutrality they said,
"How good of you to come."
Their eyes added nothing more.

Dad and I sat in the meeting area—
plain as a church kitchen.
He invited others to join us, introduced me.
They were like young pups—these patient/inmates—
so openly in need of affection.
I saw he was a favorite there among them.
"Many of the men get no visitors.
They'll be here forever," Dad told me,
"Only those with a family
get to go home."

He felt their aloneness as his own.
He made no separation between himself and them.
He was their equal, no better, just luckier
because he had us, and we did come.

He showed me handicrafts he'd made in the shop.
A clay ashtray. A wood box for cigarettes,
chewing gum, and change.

And a poem he had written:

> *Give me the heat*
> *And the dust of men*
> *Where I*
> *Can be a light*
> *all is not darkness*
> *some is day*
> *And daylight*
> *Follows night.*
> *Give me a heart*
> *Part worn with care*
> *Some grief some pleasure there*
> *And I will live*
> *As my father lived*
> *E'er though*
> *was some despair*
> *. . .*
>
> Alvin John Brandon.

He was proud of his work, and I was proud of him.
I stood humbled before his humility.

After undergoing a new series of shock treatments,
He was home for a weekend. Up early that Saturday,
seized by some mysterious inner concern,
he ran like an oversized toddler
from room to room. His plump upper body
flapping, his feet gently paddling,
he peered gleefully out each window.
Not a word was uttered.
I watched, mindful of all that he'd been through,
touched by the wonder that glowed from his face.

He came home for good mid-September.
With each hospitalization he was a little more broken.
And in truth, so were we all.

NIGHT

*7*hough scheduled to return
For my sophomore year at Western University,
and signed up to live in the sorority house
to which I'd been pledged, I got there only
to find myself in the grip
of a thousand unnameable fears.
I hadn't the will to stay.
I returned home, found work
assisting an archaeologist at the Royal Ontario Museum—
washing and labeling bones and cannonballs
unearthed in archaeological digs.
In my off-hours I began
to pursue my theater dreams.

Marilyn, also, found it
impossible to sustain interest in her studies—
she quit school and took off
for the Laurentians where
she spent the winter working and skiing.

We were bound upon a wheel of fire.

Young women with all of life ahead
but no identity to call our own.
We needed so badly to discover
who we really were.

— Early Winter '64 —

Wanting to work, to feel good about
himself, Dad tried driving a cab. But
it wasn't really suited to his nerves,
and by spring, Mum recalls:

Feeling the symptoms of illness coming on, he drove
himself to the hospital, and signed himself in.

Poor, proud battered soul.

169

— *Fall '64* —

I returned to school.
Wanting the anonymity a big school allowed,
I transferred to the University of Toronto.
Living at home was far from ideal,
but it was what I could afford.
The year I'd taken off left me
no more certain where
I was going than I had been before.

❖ ❖ ❖ ❖

— *March '65* —

came in like a lamb
and left like a lion.
April showed its cruelty.

Dad's illness reappeared
just as I began studying for end-of-year exams.
His moods made it impossible to concentrate at home.
So I camped out with a band of friends
at the school library.
Without that cluster of benign outlaws
I don't know if I'd have made it through.
In fact I managed a "B" average that year,
and got my tuition paid for the next.

Summer was a complete nightmare.
Dad's paranoid accusations and fantasies
had us living *The Glass Menagerie*.
I wanted to shout like Tom:

> *Yes, I'm going to opium dens,*
> *dens of vice, and criminal hangouts.*
> *. . . I carry a tommy gun in a violin case.*
> *. . . You ugly babbling old (man).*

Marilyn and I decided to move out.
We packed up, took the bus and streetcar downtown.
We were now twenty and twenty-one years old, but
images of us at four and five,
nine and ten flashed through my mind.
We were moving once again.

Walking the streets
in the vicinity of the University of Toronto,
we knocked at the first sign of a ROOM FOR LET.
The landlady looked at us long and hard.
We told her we were students, moving downtown
to be close to school when it opened.

Recognizing the orphans we were,
she took us in.

As we climbed up the two flights of unlit stairs to the attic,
I felt the weight of responsibility descend.
The future smelled dank.

We were there only a day or two when Dad
called begging us to come home.
"He's been up all night crying," Mum pleaded.
I remember him arriving to get us,
his body shaking, his face so sad.

       Tears do scald like molten lead.

We were dutiful daughters really, so we
readily agreed to return.

He was struggling to hold on, but he was
a prisoner of his own mine field:
explosions within and around him
occurred without warning. Soon again,
we were mother and children—
the innocent victims of
his manic blasts.

He bought a sporty, siren red MG.
Taking off many a night after midnight,
rubber squealing and burning as he spun out the drive.

Many an hour did I lay awake shuddering, wondering —
what if he took a suicide curve?

There were few things Dad cherished more
than he did Suzanne.
That he loved us all I have no doubt,
but she was the only one
toward whom he bore not a minute's malice.

So, when early that September
the paranoid delusion hit

172

that Suzanne was to be kidnapped by the Mafia,
he had no choice (I suppose) but to protect her.

He drove up to Burhamthorpe Collegiate, demanding
the principal hand her over.

> "The Mafia's after me," he said,
> "For some fine art paintings I bought.
> They're threatening to take my precious daughter,
> Suzanne, to retrieve them."

The principal—an astute observer—
knew right away Dad was a madman,
and called the police.
One, two, three—
he had him committed.
What was impossible for us
was routine and easy for him.

The hospital records tell the tale:
September 17, 1965:

> *Mr. Brandon was brought to the hospital under Section 28-
> A-1, and certified under Section 22 . . .*

> *Well known to hospital from at least 3 other admissions. . .
> Discharged last year after 2 month stay, seen in follow-up
> interviews until end of November '64. Dropped out of our
> sight sometime around end of January. . . Present clinical
> condition more severe than it has been, and the patient has
> been rather belligerent, and the delusions more bizarre
> than on previous occasions. He feels to be threatened more
> immediately, and had been physically aggressive toward
> other patients whom he suspected of being a member in
> different illegal organizations . . .*

Release this time came only
with an iron-clad two year probation —
if Dad failed to go in weekly for consultation,
failed to stay on his medication,
the doctor warned:

"You'll be rehospitalized
immediately and risk being
locked up the rest of your days."

Harsh as the agreement was, Dad signed,
and kept to his word. Like a chastened schoolboy
he went down every week, always staying
a few hours—visiting, playing cards
with the men he'd made friends with while in.
There was one "baby" man he'd even occasionally
bring back with him for a "weekend at home."

Dad was trying with all he had
to live a normal life.
As Mum says:
> It took a lot of strength on his part. He wasn't a lazy man.
> He was anxious to get out and do some work. It wasn't
> easy, but he finally did get a job, as a messenger with a
> stock brokerage firm. The first week was so hard. We'd
> leave together in the morning. He was so nervous, his face
> beaded with sweat. He'd sit close beside me on the
> streetcar, not saying much, but I could feel him thinking.

She was his mother, always.

Dad stayed with that lowly job,
never missing a day for the next five years.
It was all he had left of his pride.
My respect for him grew stronger every day,
every year he endured.

Of the aftermath Mum says:
> When he got on his medication it was an entirely different
> life. It did tend to drain all his energy, but that was better
> than having a wild man around.

This truth was our most bitter pill.

NIGHT

I'd have given anything
To see him vitally active, happy once again.
I harbored a Heidi-like fantasy —

> *if I could just provide him a mountaintop retreat,*
> *where his basic needs are met,*
> *might he rage rage rage to the wind, and find release?*

Of course that was never to be.
I asked him once if he thought
the treatments he'd received had helped.
To my surprise he answered:
        "Yes, it was as if I was drunk on emotion.
        I had no control."
I asked, "How does the medication make you feel?"
He said simply:
        "I feel everything I ever felt, I just can't act."

From this point on
his was the aspect of a man in a psychic shroud.
What could and did bring a glimmer to
his sad, so sad, brown eyes
were letters he'd receive in response to his
"Poem of the Nations."

> *Why seek we now*
> *Odd blending still*
> *With doubt and some duress*
> *We share the task*
> *To unravel here*
> *The worldly needs that bless.*
>   . . . .

He still sent that poem out as
the spirit moved him.
("If the spirit moves me"—
that was a favorite phrase of his,
a phrase that brought with it
a twinkle to his eye and a soft gentle
smile to his lips.)

He enjoyed receiving the
token letters of gratitude
that came thanking him
for sending that poem,
one even personally signed by
Martin Luther King, Jr.

❖ ❖ ❖ ❖

Simultaneous with Dad's last hospitalization
I was entering my senior graduating year.

And,
I got a job—my first professional role—
playing Cinderella—(fancy that!)—
with a children's theater troupe;
I did four performances a weekend:
at five dollars a show, that made twenty—
with a little additional help from Mum,
I moved downtown.

Dad's illness was a warning.
I thought, "If only he'd received treatment earlier,
maybe things would have been different."
Wanting to understand,
worried that I might become ill like him,
I placed myself in psychoanalysis.

There I met with Dr. X twice a week.
He took a "classic" approach:
with silent imperturbability
he rung out of me an intense rage,
and an onslaught of blame.

I directed all my hostilities at him personally,
and the more silently he endured,
the sharper were my attacks.

I never did understand
what I deemed to be his
refusal to defend himself.
How, I wondered, could he just sit there
listening to me rail on as mightily as I did?
His silence acted as a provocation, and
I eagerly met the challenge.

I know now—Dr. X's granite endurance
allowed me to displace the full spectrum of my anger,
anger I would never dream of expressing fully in real life.
I freely attacked and blamed the psychiatric world
and its pharmacology for the semi-vegetative state
in which Dad would live the last years of his life.

For me the price the medication exacted—
the price of his and our peace—was entirely too great.
And Dr. X became the whipping post for this gripe.

About six months into the analysis
Dr. X informed me he would be giving up
one-to-one patient care, and going into research.
I was to be transferred to Dr. Y.
I joked that my ranting had surely driven him
to seek a more abstract path.

Changing doctors didn't disturb me particularly.
In fact, I was glad to be free of Dr. X
as I was a little ashamed of the active aggression
his person and methods elicited. And,
Dr. Y as it happened, was someone
for whom I felt an immediate fondness.
(It reminds me now, as I think, a little
of the move from Grade One to Grade Two,
when I'd screamed, cried, and resisted the first teacher,
then quietly opened my heart to the next.)

Dr. Y's attentive silences
provided me a fluid, placid pool
in which to concentrate and reflect
as I told my story.

Out of the blue, he interrupted to
toss in a word or two:
instantly, my train of thought
dispersed, spun and reformed.
I saw life entirely anew.
He met me in the realm of myth
(where I so longed to "play")—
telling me I reminded him
of Anouilh's Antigone:

> *Little Antigone has been caught—and handcuffed.*
> *She can be herself at last.*

Yes, yes!
And, he encouraged my ambitions
To act.

> *Have the courage to fan the spark into a flame.*

❖ ❖ ❖ ❖

Dad died of cancer in July 1973.

It was a long, slow, painful death.

The first cancer struck about 1967—
eating at his intestines, colon, rectum.
The treatment? A colostomy—
a bag for the waste as
he could no longer naturally eliminate.

Five years later the liver went.

By late 1972 he was
little more than ravaged skin and bone.
Pain-killers granted hallucinations as relief.
He was grateful, came to cherish those pictures,
calling them "My painted desert."

NIGHT

Early 1973 it became necessary
to hospitalize him once again.
Dad knew he was dying and
desperately wanted to remain at home.
Of his two most ardent requests
only one could be granted.
"Never abandon me to institutional care," he pleaded.
"If I must die, let me die at home. And please,
don't lay me out in a closed coffin; before you bury me
be certain I am really dead."

He gave form to his fears
in a poem, *The Retarded Child*, writing in the first person

> *There wasn't time*
> *for boys like me*
> *We were better away*
> *No one could see*
>
> *Strange things went on*
> *I couldn't recall*
> *A bed now empty*
> *Down the hall*
> . . .
> *I can't speak much*
> *I do think dumb*
> *Strange buggies are fine*
> *But I need Mum*
> . . .

If she could have, I know
Mum would have kept him home,
but his insurance dollars had run out.
It was impossible for her to work and provide
the twenty-four hour attention Dad needed.
Too weak to walk, and physically incapable of
performing the most basic of functions for himself,
there was little choice—
Mum had to make the hard decision,
the decision which would again awaken
his scorn and blame-filled wrath.

179

What hubris lay in his undying inability to forgive?
Would the trumpet sound for him on the other side?

For a good six months more his heart
refused to give up.
Flesh and muscle all but disappeared,
His once large powerful limbs now
long talons of bone.

Over the course of the months before he died
Mum, Marilyn, and Suzanne paid
the daily visits, provided the
hands-on comfort and care.

Living in New York, I really couldn't
get to see him, but I phoned regularly, and
lived to hear him smile at the sound of my voice.

> *The weight of this sad time we must obey,*
> *Speak what we feel, not what we ought to say.*

I wrote him many a letter and poem,
In one I asked:

> *Did you see the paradise*
> *Where I nurtured you,*
> *And named you King?*
> *Where I fed you milk and honey,*
> *And celebrated your divinity*
> *When the sun shone in the morning?*

> *Did you hear my voice resound in anger*
> *When they bound you in the chains of*
> *Their paralyzed morality?*
> *Did you see my lips run dry,*
> *And my tears fall*

> *When you smiled, and*
> *Recognized me as your child?*

180

NIGHT

I knew he had,
and when he died
my account with him was clear.

❖ ❖ ❖ ❖

One night, years after his death, I'd just gone to bed;
I was lying there drifting in that place between
wakefulness and dream when
I felt a warm, softly palpable vibration hovering near my face.
I knew immediately it was Dad.
I felt completely comfortable in the experience,
his presence—peaceful, safe, unafraid.
We greeted one another fondly, and I asked him
how he was doing. He answered, saying,

> *I'm fine, I'm taking a good rest.*
> *It'll be a very long time before I choose Life again.*

I completely understood.

Dolores as Antigone, in "Women of Ancient Greece,"
New York City, 1971-72.

Dawn

$\mathcal{D}$ad's illness was his most resounding legacy:
it gave as much as it took.
Every day of our family life required a personal adjustment
to his overwhelming, darkly marvelous presence.
We laughed and cried at his command.
For better, for worse—
his illness and the domestic conflict it spawned
forever shape the prism through which I view my life.

And when he died, of course, he wasn't dead.
He lives in every cell of my body, just as
do Mum, Mémère and Pépère,
Ma, Marilyn and Suzanne.
Their silences shape my face and eyes,
Their stubbornness is grit in my teeth,
Our separateness occupies my afternoons.
My chest sifts each wound.

❖ ❖ ❖ ❖

Although I came of age in the bitter hours of night, the
ambitions I held for my adulthood were stored in the sweet
seeds of music scattered and sown in the morning.

Forever will I hear

> *Connais-tu le pays où fleurit*
> *l'oranger? Le pays des fruits*
> *d'or et des roses vermeilles,*

Always that song
    That voice
        That tongue.

> *Connais-tu la maison où l'on*
> *m'attend là-bas?*
> *La salle aux lambris d'or, où des hommes*
> *de marbre M'appelent*
> *dans la nuit en me tendant les bras?*

Yes, I know the room, Maman.
where the setting sun
casts rays of gold
and Daddy's arms still call
to me in the night

> *Et la cour où l'on danse*
> *à l'ombre d'un grand arbre?*
> *Et le lac transparent où glissent*
> *sur les eaux Mille bateaux légers*
> *pareils à des oiseaux!*

Yes,
I dance in the shadows
of that great tree that is
you and Daddy

> *Hélas!*

186

DAWN

I never forget you.
que ne puis-je te suivre
Vers ce pays lointain d'où □
le sort m'exila!

That voice forms the lotus of my yearnings.

From my parents and grandparents I inherited
a talent for the dramatic, and an impulse to write.
Through their love I was led to poetry and
the literature of opera and theater where
I found the stories that helped me understand
what I have lived through.

The day Dad died I was leading the Chorus
in an off-off-Broadway production of Euripedes' "Medea."
Medea, another star-crossed love story.
Mignon, Delilah, Micaela—
now she. A story in which
the real victims are wholly innocent children.

> "*. . . Many things the gods achieve beyond*
> *our judgment. What we thought is not confirmed*
> *and what we thought not God contrives.*"

And so it happened once
                    and will happen again
                                        to me.

❖ ❖ ❖ ❖

Jim Thompson, 1960s.

DAWN

- 1 -

Within a year of Dad's death
despite genuine love I left
my first husband, Bill (a fine, dear man, artist),
whom I now love like a brother.

I left for a new love, Jim—
a teacher, a streetcorner crooner;
a varsity basketball star.
A gentle, joyous hard drinker;
African-American, deeply devoted
to the civil rights struggle of his people.

Appalled and without laying eyes on him—
"How could you?" Mum insisted.
"My family, my friends
they'll never approve!
I might as well die!
You are no longer my child!"

> *Shame is inherited.*
> *It lived in my forebears,*
> *it lives in me*

Likewise, at first sight of my picture on his bedroom table,
Jim's stepmother packed his clothes, wailing
"Get out! Don't ever come back.
Go live in that white world."
Every aspect of his presence was removed
from the room in her home that had been his,
every trophy he'd ever won was dismantled,
every proud photograph was removed,
every belonging hoarded, and hidden;
on the walls she hung
pictures of black women crying.

On his job women hitherto indifferent
berated and accused, "You betrayed us.
You're another good black man lost."
When his father attempted to

189

oppose her and accept us,
Jim's stepmother threatened a divorce.

My rage took flight in words—
words I wrote down and mailed to her:

> *Just try to do something true and honest*
> *in your life—*
> *that's when they'll crucify you*
> *make a pariah of you,*
> *stick a knife in your heart.*
>
> *Then will you know pain:*
> *pain that will destroy you*
> *if you are not vigilant and strong.*
>
> *And their eyes look at you*
> *eyes full of hate and greed;*
> *and they plead their honor*
> *denying you yours.*
> *They plead their love—*
>
> *love full of judgment*
> *love full of fear*
> *love full of boundaries,*
> *limitations that strangle and*
> *choke every song you want to sing.*
>
> *They embrace you calling you "child"*
> *And kiss you trying to suck from you*
> *your body and your mind*
> *because without you*
> *they cannot live.*
>
> *And they're living in you and through you*
> *so long as you are willing to be their prisoner.*
> *But just try to fly—*

190

DAWN

they'll shoot arrows at your heart,
they'll bind your mind
and shackle your feet
and inflict such torture on you
your screams and tears are useless

for no one is listening.
To kill you they cannot listen
to you—the victim.

They cannot look into your eyes,
they will not feel the trembling of your limbs.

Mother father, no! Oh no!
Do not look at me when you kill me
for in me you will not see
your hate reflected
you'll see only the babe
you say you desired in love.
But you did not desire me,
you desired only yourself.
You bore me out of your own pain.

No, oh no
Do not look at me when you kill me!
Look at yourself!
Do it in front of a mirror so
you can see your own terror, your insanity;
the blood green of your face,
the claws you thought were fingers.

See yourself in all your darkness
and scream for me to help you,
to rescue you from the nightmare of your existence.
For I could never do to you
what you are doing to me.
If you would cry out to me
you might feel my body melting in the heat of your hate.
And you might seek to drown in my waters,

seek to squelch the blood yellow flames
shooting from you—
flames so out of control. And maybe
you would realize in my truth Beauty
beyond anything you have ever, ever dreamed—

a Beauty full of light and air
a Beauty so much greater than you or I.

Utterly lost—

Ino sent mad, and made to wander . . .

I aborted two pregnancies within
the first six months of our love.

Blamed Dad

Shame is a mermaid
her sex vilified
her life-giving organs amputated

And wrote of
my sorrow.

Mother, mother
I am crying
Mother, mother,
I am dying

Where is the flower that bloomed
in my belly so strong?
Where is the flower?
Oh, where is she gone?

Mother, mother
Are you listening?
Mother, mother
When's the christening?
Where is the love
that bloomed in my belly so strong?

DAWN

Where is the love?
Oh where is she gone?

Gone! Twice, oh twice
she is gone!

Mother white,
Mother black,
Mother morning,
Mother night.
Mother, mothers!
Give up your hatred?
Mothers pray for the dead

Grandbabies aborted—
Dreamt only, never known!

Our tears were heavy with blood.
There was no new race born here.

Forever do I hear

Connais-tu le pays où fleurit
l'oranger? Le pays des fruits
d'or et des roses vermeilles,

Always that song
    That voice
        That tongue.

Connais-tu la maison où l'on
m'attend là-bas?
La salle aux lambris d'or, où des hommes
de marbre M'appelent
dans la nuit en me tendant les bras?

Yes, I know the house, Maman.
Like you I am in exile
so far from my home.

Et la cour où l'on danse
à l'ombre d'un grand arbre?
Et le lac transparent où glissent
sur les eaux Mille bateaux légers
pareils à des oiseaux!

Hélas!
I will never forget you.
que ne puis-je te suivre
Vers ce pays lointain d'où•
le sort m'exila!

C'est là, c'est là que je
voudrais vivre, Aimer, aimer et mourir!
C'est là que je voudrais vivre, c'est là,
oui, c'est là!

Oui, c'est là.

I go with you in life
I go with you in love
I go with you in death.

Shame is the shattering of glass,
A head smashed through.
Shame is a mother's black eye.
Shame is blood on white cotton panties.

Now

Shame is a black man crying.

❖ ❖ ❖ ❖

Jim Thompson and Dolores Brandon, 1970s.

Jim Thompson and Dolores Brandon Wedding,
November 1979

DAWN

- 2 -

> *Like anemone, we are easily stripped*
> *of our petals in the wind.*

For two years after I moved in with Jim
Mum refused to see me or speak. Then—
one day she wrote:

> *I dreamt of you last night;*
> *you looked so beautiful in a lovely yellow dress.*
> *It's so long since I've seen you.*

For the next eight years I visited her on my own
every February for her birthday.
And I wrote:

> *We talk on long distance telephone—but*
> *you don't remove your veils—and*
> *you ask me to wear a mask when*
> *I am with you.*
> *So many chances for intimacy have been*
> *missed, deliberately denied.*
> *We no longer share communion.*

Ten years passed before Mum agreed to meet Jim.
Ten years I asked no one for help,
I was complicit. Seeking
to protect her I gave in to her fears.
Ten years I accepted a role of her choosing.
Ten years . . .

It was all too difficult to comprehend.
Each of us—Jim and I—
we'd always counted our mothers
among our best friends.
What happened?
We hadn't changed.
We thought we'd become the people
our mothers brought us up to become.

197

We were children of the '60s; we believed
in the civil rights dream.

We wished to be as Melanie sang:

> candles in the rain
> to be there is to remember
> lay it down again
> lay down
> lay down
> lay it down again
> men can live as brothers
> candles in the rain

Jim's face reflects the deep soul of black folk,
and, with his prematurely greying hair and beard,
people on the street take him
for Frederick Douglass reincarnate.
Children smile when they see him.
He's the Pied Piper of Fort Green.

I, nascent actress and writer,
had the good fortune to meet Anaïs Nin.
She became the mother of my soul.
In a letter she wrote:

> *I am adopting you to replace your mother.*
> *I love you both for transcending absurd boundaries.*

❖ ❖ ❖ ❖

DAWN

- 3 -

Five years into our being together,
November 16, 1979,
Jim and I did marry, but
we never did have children.
Yes, I viewed pregnancy with the compound eyes of terror.
But was I afraid of giving birth
to a child who might look different than me?
Never, no, not for one instant!

Pregnant, I imagined holding
a dark-skinned baby in my arms;
taking a little brown boy's hand in my own.
These thoughts pleased me very much.

> *Fragile child—*
> *Neptune's bounty,*
> *golden seashell,*
> *washed by the waves of a transcendent desire;*
> *formed yet formless,*
> *jewel of a thousand uncut facets—*
> *where is your home?*

❖ ❖ ❖ ❖

- 4 -

In the eleventh year of this exile,
my sister Suzanne announced her plans to marry,
Mum threatened not to attend the wedding.
I recognized the refusal as her idea of Justice:
she felt bound to treat each daughter the same.

I decided enough's enough and wrote to Aunt Jul
telling her of the sad, secret strife.
The letter she wrote in reply was all and more
than I could ever have wished for:

> *Dear Dolores,*
>
> *As I read and reread your letter, I learned so many things—I was unaware of so many things—and there are so many things I do not understand. In your letter you refer to being disowned, being rejected, your life being shameful, you've made sacrifices to protect your mum, receive nothing but criticism . . .*
>
> *My heart aches at the thought you are enduring such inner hardships and pain and sorrow.*
>
> *You must believe me Dolores, you have nothing to be ashamed of, absolutely nothing, nothing to feel guilty about, nothing to regret, and your life has not been shameful...*

Julienne then took it upon
herself to write:

> *Ma chère Jeanne:*
> *J'ai quelque chose à te demander . . .*

Yes, I had something to ask . . .

With compassion and grace she told Mum of the confidences I'd shared. She asked her to accept Jim into our family.

DAWN

Maman et papa nous ont enseigné
ces choses dès le bas age . . .

Maman and Papa taught us
to accept people of all races.

The letter was four pages long.
She recalled the black teenage boys

    . . . Bill, Jeremy, Joshua, Glenn and Stan

whom (when she and Mum were children)
Pépère would hire to help him on the farm—
youngsters who were always welcome
friends at supper.

Jul wanted to see us all reunited, and
what better time but Suzanne's wedding.
Mum was persuaded and agreed.
The wedding took place at
the National Arboretum in Washington, D.C.
Suzanne was the only one of Mum's girls
to marry wearing a formal white wedding gown
(the only one who would give her a grandchild—Emily).
Mum couldn't have been more cordial to Jim.
He approached her softly saying,
"I'm so nervous meeting you."
With tenderness, even awe,
her placid blue eyes gazed steadily at his dark brown face.
She took his hand gently and responded,

                    "Oh?"

We thought we'd crossed the divide,
but:
        Shame is a spider:
        Her blood runs in the veins of our blushes

        Shame leaves a sticky trail in the mind

That December when I asked
"May we spend Christmas with you at home?"
Without much hesitation, she uttered a definitive "No."
Three more years passed before she was ready
for that and then
it had to be imposed.
"We're coming, we'll stay at a hotel!"

On Jim's side, the story was practically the same.
There were eight years without a "Hi there,"
"Happy Birthday," or "How are you?"

Only the death of a paternal uncle prompted them to call.
Then, as his stepmother will graciously acknowledge,
we entered the half-open door *as gently as butterflies.*

It was a fragile truce.
Jim could get no one to talk, to really own up
to the pain of the lost eight years.
Genuine dialogue was laughed off or shunned.

> *Shame is a festering sore*

When Pop (Jim's dad) died—a brittle three years later—
no place was reserved for me in the family funeral pew. So,
Jim and I sat together in a back row of the church
and rode with friends to the cemetery behind
the limousine-led motorcade. Once there,
stepmother, sister, and brother huddled together
extending not a hand, not an arm,
not one comforting glance;
just their grieving bowed backs
did they turn to Jim.

> *Shame is a repetition compulsion*
> *Shame leaves you naked when*
> *others are clothed*

Bitterness reached its peak on that day.

202

Dolores Brandon as Elena in
THE END OF WAR by Karen Malpede 1977

I decided there and then
no family member would ever again
get the chance to turn their back on us.

I'd rarely visit Jim's family again.

- *5* -

  I am the mutablilis rose,
  variegated, adaptable—actress

I found mothers and daughters,
fathers and daughters,
sisters, brothers and sisters
in every role I played on the stage.

Cinderella, Velma Sparrow,
Yerma, the Bride in Blood Wedding,
Anya, Antigone, Electra,
and Cassandra, who warned:

  ". . . the shame is better left in silence, for fear
  my singing voice become the voice of wretchedness."

Each character in her own way was like me—
determined to break free of her past.

Rebirthing occured.
I found new ways to walk and talk,
new ways to think.

  I am the song I wanted to sing
  I am the dance
  Floating feather, water lily—
  Child woman of the sea.

Each role a palimpsest
for the living of a primal yearning, a longing
that would never be erased—

DAWN

Ever that song
that voice
that tongue.

> *Printemps qui commence,*
> *Portant l'espérance*
> *Aux coeurs amoureux,*

So spring begins,
and hope lives

> *Ton souffle qui passe*
> *De la terre efface*
> *Les jours malheureux.*
> *Tout brûle en notre âme*
> *Et ta douce flamme*
> *Vient sécher nos pleurs;*

Breath passes
over the earth
wipes away
sad days.
Everything burns
in my soul

> *Tu rends à la terre,*
> *Par un doux mystère,*
> *Les fruits et les fleurs.*
> *En vain je suis belle!*

Alas,
in vain I am beautiful.
The career I'd wanted so desperately
I did not sustain.
I lost faith
in myself

THE ROOT IS BITTER, THE ROOT IS SWEET

Give me the roses they call Wine Cup,
Magic Lantern, Snowbird, Nightingale,
Tipsey Imperial Concubine,
Joyfulness, Sweet Fancy.
Keep those named for royals or celebs.

Please,
don't strain to hear why,
there will be no could be's would
be's what if's spoken here.

Only—
this story keeps begging to be told.

An exquisite silken filament;
it spins as the zephyr breathes
a silver song.

In the shadow of each sentence written
here is a story initiates know—
the Persephone Demeter journey
turned inside out.

In the shadow of each word
is the story of a mother and daughter,
discovering what's been lost,
recovering what was denied.

Like algae on the surface of a great lake
robs the body of precious nutrition
leaving other life forms to starve,
so Dad's illness abducted my mother.

In the act of my asking her questions,
questions that took us back
through the hours and days
of our morning, noon and night,
we reclaimed our love.

With the telling of this story
she heard my anger and sorrow,
her tears asked forgiveness

the veils are drawn
the masks are removed
intimacy is achieved
communion is once again shared.

- 6 -

*I*t took twenty years, but
today Mum and Jim
find genuine delight in each other's company.

Jim, of course, never had a chance to meet my father,
but on one visit "home" we went with Mum and Marilyn
to plant chrysanthemums at Dad's grave.
Digging in the hard, dry soil, Jim unearthed a stone—
a stone in the shape of a heart.

That stone fit perfectly in the palm of his hand.

Translations

- from the French by Suzanne Shayt -

- Lyrics from "Mignon" by Ambroise Thomas -

Do you know the country where
the orange tree blossoms?
The country of golden fruit and vermillion roses?

Where the breeze is softer and the bird lighter,
where bees gather nectar all year long?

Where an eternal spring beams and smiles like a
blessing from God
under an ever-blue sky!
Alas!

Why can't I follow you to this happy shore from where fate
banished me.

It's there! It's there where I would like
to live, to love, and to die!
It's there where I would like to live,
It's there! Yes it's there!

Do you know the house where they are waiting over there?
The golden paneled room, where marble men call my name
in the night stretching out their arms to me?

And the courtyard where they dance
in the shadow of a tall tree?
And the transparent lake where
a thousand light boats
glide over the water like birds!

Alas!

Why can't I follow you
to this far-off country from where
fate banished me!

It's there, it's there where I would like to live,
to love, to love, and to die!

It's there where I would like, to live,
it's there, yes it's there!
Yes, it's there.

- "Delilah" (from Samson & Delilah by Saint Saens) -

Spring who begins by carrying
hope to loving hearts,
Your breath which passes over the earth
wipes away sad days.
Everything burns in our soul, and your soft
flame comes to dry our tears;

You give back to the earth, by a gentle
mystery, the fruit and flowers.

In vain I am beautiful!

My heart full of love, lamenting
the unfaithful, awaits his return!
Living on hope, my distressed heart
remembers former happiness.

At nightfall I will go a sad lover,
to sit and wait for him
in a flood of tears driving away my sorrow,
if he comes back some day, for him my fondness,
and gentle rapture, as a burning love watches out for his return.

Driving away my sorrow, if he comes back some
day, for him my fondness and gentle rapture as a burning love
watches out for his return!

- Prayer -

Hail Mary, mother of God, pray for
us sinners, now, and at the hour of our death. Amen.

- *Micaela's song from CARMEN* -

I say, that nothing is afflicting me
I say, alas! I can vouch for myself;
but whenever I try to be brave, at the bottom of
my heart I am dying of fright!
Alone in this wild place, all alone I am afraid; but
I am wrong to be afraid; you will give me courage,
you will protect me Lord!

Acknowledgements

Grateful acknowledgement to the Hal Leonard Corp-oration for permission to use the following:

> The Inch Worm
> from the Motion Picture *Hans Christian Andersen*
> By Frank Loesser
> © 1951, 1952 (Renewed) *Frank Music Corp.*
> All Rights Reserved

> The Ugly Duckling
> from the Motion Picture *Hans Christian Andersen*
> By Frank Loesser
> © 1951, 1952 (Renewed) *Frank Music Corp.*
> All Rights Reserved

> Anywhere I Wander
> from the Motion Picture *Hans Christian Andersen*
> By Frank Loesser
> © 1951, 1952 (Renewed) *Frank Music Corp.*
> All Rights Reserved

Grateful acknowledgement to Thomas Allen & Son, Limited for permission to use the two Edna Jaques poems in "Beside Still Waters," both published in Canada by Thomas Allen & Son, Limited.

Grateful acknowledgement is made to editors and publishers of magazines in which some of the poems in this book first appeared: a modified version of "Summer as it Was" appeared in *Branching Out: a Canadian magazine for women*, Volume V, No. 1, 1978, and "Oh my dear Ma" first appeared in *Sistersong: Women Across Cultures*, Fall 1996.

❖ ❖ ❖ ❖

Source Notes

A Long Day's Journey into Night
Eugene O'Neil

Antigone
Jean Anouilh

Death of a Salesman
Arthur Miller

Dr. Jeckyll and Mr. Hyde
Robert Louis Stevenson

Folk Songs

King Lear
Wm. Shakespeare

Latin Proverb

Medea
Euripedes

Personal journals of Dolores Brandon

The Holy Bible

The Glass Menagerie
Tennessee Williams

The Trojan Women
Euripedes

Various children's nursery rhymes

❖ ❖ ❖ ❖

www.ingramcontent.com/pod-product-compliance
Lightning Source LLC
Chambersburg PA
CBHW070411270326
41926CB00014B/2783